Gallifrey's Yule Logs

Gallifrey's Yule Logs

Matthew Petchinsky

Gallifrey's Yule Logs: A Festive Doctor Who Cookbook
By: Matthew Petchinsky

Disclaimer:

This is a **fan-made cookbook** created as a holiday celebration inspired by the universe of *Doctor Who*. It is not affiliated with, endorsed by, or connected to the BBC or its license holders. All characters, settings, and elements of *Doctor Who* are the property of the BBC. This book is an imaginative, festive tribute for fans—offered in the spirit of creativity and joy.

Happy Holidays! ◈ ◈

Introduction

Welcome to a culinary journey through time and space!

Whether you're a Time Lord, a companion, or just a devoted fan of *Doctor Who*, this guide is your TARDIS to a world of imaginative and festive holiday cooking. From the snowy peaks of the Ood-Sphere to the warmth of Earth-bound Christmases, food has always been a powerful way to connect with the spirit of the season. But why settle for ordinary holiday meals when you can add a touch of Gallifreyan magic and intergalactic flavor to your celebrations?

The holidays are a time of gathering, sharing, and storytelling, and there's no better way to bring people together than with a feast that bridges universes. This book will take you on an exploration of festive traditions from Gallifrey and beyond, blending the timeless essence of Earth's holiday cheer with the otherworldly wonders of the *Doctor Who* universe. Imagine sitting down to a table adorned with delicacies inspired by the Great Houses of Gallifrey, sweet treats from the Forest of Cheem, or hearty dishes fit for a feast on the Starship Titanic.

The Festive Traditions of Gallifrey and Beyond

While the Time Lords of Gallifrey were often depicted as stoic and steeped in formality, they were not without their own celebrations. This guide pays homage to their rich, ceremonial culture by reimagining what Gallifreyan holiday traditions might look like. Picture a banquet under the twin suns, with tables laden with delicacies that blend ancient Gallifreyan customs and futuristic flair.

But Gallifrey is only the beginning. Across the universe, from the bustling markets of New Earth to the frozen shores of Trenzalore, every planet has its own unique way of celebrating. The Daleks may not be known for their hospitality, but their relentless precision could inspire the perfect soufflé. And while the Cybermen might prefer upgrades to recipes, their efficiency might just help you streamline your holiday preparations. Every chapter in this guide invites you to explore these fantastical locales through the lens of food, offering you creative ways to bring their essence into your kitchen.

How to Add a *Doctor Who* Twist to Your Holiday Cooking

This book isn't just about recipes—it's about embracing the whimsy, adventure, and boundless creativity of *Doctor Who*. Each dish has been crafted to evoke the spirit of the show while staying accessible for chefs of all skill levels.

For those new to cooking, think of this as your sonic screwdriver for the kitchen—an all-purpose tool to unlock culinary magic. For seasoned cooks, consider these recipes as inspiration to regenerate your usual holiday menu into something truly extraordinary.

Here's what you can expect:

- **Gallifreyan Elegance:** Sophisticated dishes with a nod to the Time Lords, featuring intricate flavors and techniques to impress any guest.
- **Earth with a Twist:** Classic holiday recipes reimagined with alien influences, blending comfort food with adventurous flair.
- **Intergalactic Fun:** Playful, easy-to-make treats inspired by *Doctor Who* icons like the TARDIS, Daleks, and the Weeping Angels.
- **Festive Drinks:** Signature cocktails and beverages to toast the season in true Whovian style.

This guide also includes tips on presentation and décor to transform your dining space into a festive celebration worthy of a Christmas Special. Whether it's a TARDIS centerpiece or Dalek-shaped cookies, your holiday table will become the ultimate conversation starter.

Traveling Through Time and Space in the Kitchen

Cooking is an adventure, much like piloting the TARDIS. There will be moments of trial and error, unexpected surprises, and, hopefully, plenty of delight. But that's the beauty of this journey—it's not just about the destination but the joy of creating something special along the way.

So, grab your apron and your sense of wonder, and let's embark on a festive culinary adventure through time and space. From Gallifrey to Earth and every dimension in between, your kitchen is about to become the most exciting place in the universe. Allons-y!

Chapter 1: The Doctor's Favorite Tea Cakes

Tea and biscuits have always held a special place in the heart of the Doctor. Whether it's sharing a cuppa with a companion or taking a moment of solace between daring escapades, these simple pleasures represent comfort, tradition, and a connection to humanity. In this chapter, we explore the Doctor's love for tea and biscuits with recipes that pay homage to this quintessentially British tradition, infused with the whimsy of Gallifrey.

The Legacy of Tea and Biscuits in *Doctor Who*

From the Eleventh Doctor's love for Jammie Dodgers to the Tenth Doctor's penchant for a good cup of tea, this humble pairing has appeared time and time again throughout the series. For the Doctor, tea and biscuits serve as a reminder of Earth's enduring charm—a small but meaningful pleasure amidst the chaos of time and space. Inspired by these moments, this chapter features a selection of recipes designed to evoke the warmth and nostalgia of a cozy teatime, with a distinctly Gallifreyan twist.

Gallifreyan Honey-Infused Tea Cakes

These delicate tea cakes are inspired by the rich ceremonial culture of Gallifrey, where honey was said to symbolize the eternal golden glow of the planet's twin suns. Infused with floral notes and a hint of cosmic spice, these tea cakes are the perfect accompaniment to a pot of Earl Grey or a steaming mug of peppermint tea.

Ingredients:

For the tea cakes:

- 1 ½ cups all-purpose flour
- 1 tsp baking powder
- ½ tsp baking soda
- ¼ tsp salt
- ½ cup unsalted butter, softened
- ¾ cup Gallifreyan honey (or a high-quality floral honey as a substitute)
- 2 large eggs
- ½ tsp vanilla extract
- ½ tsp ground cardamom
- ⅓ cup buttermilk

For the glaze:

- ½ cup powdered sugar
- 3 tbsp Gallifreyan honey
- 2 tbsp freshly brewed tea (Earl Grey or chamomile recommended)
- Edible gold dust (optional, for a touch of Gallifreyan elegance)

Instructions:
Step 1: Prepare the Tea Cake Batter

1. Preheat your oven to 350°F (175°C) and grease a muffin tin or tea cake mold.
2. In a medium bowl, sift together the flour, baking powder, baking soda, and salt. Set aside.
3. In a large mixing bowl, beat the softened butter and honey together until light and fluffy, about 2-3 minutes.
4. Add the eggs one at a time, beating well after each addition. Mix in the vanilla extract and ground cardamom.
5. Gradually add the dry ingredients to the wet mixture in three parts, alternating with the buttermilk. Begin and end with the dry ingredients. Mix until just combined; do not overmix.

Step 2: Bake the Tea Cakes

1. Spoon the batter evenly into the prepared muffin tin or molds, filling each about two-thirds full.
2. Bake for 15-18 minutes, or until a toothpick inserted into the center comes out clean.
3. Allow the tea cakes to cool in the pan for 5 minutes, then transfer them to a wire rack to cool completely.

Step 3: Make the Glaze

1. In a small bowl, whisk together the powdered sugar, honey, and brewed tea until smooth and slightly runny. Adjust the consistency with more tea or sugar as needed.
2. Once the tea cakes are completely cool, drizzle the glaze over the top using a spoon or piping bag.

Step 4: Add a Gallifreyan Touch

- For an extra special presentation, lightly dust the glazed tea cakes with edible gold dust to mimic the shimmering glow of Gallifrey's twin suns.

Tips for the Perfect Tea Cakes

- **Gallifreyan Honey Substitution:** If you can't access a local Gallifreyan market (and who can?), opt for lavender, acacia, or wildflower honey for a similar delicate floral flavor.
- **Spice Variations:** Try adding a pinch of cinnamon or nutmeg for a warmer flavor profile, reminiscent of the Doctor's adventures in snowy climates.
- **Mold Matters:** Use traditional tea cake molds or mini bundt pans for an elegant look, or stick with muffin tins for a more casual presentation.

Pairing Suggestions

The key to enjoying these tea cakes is pairing them with the right tea. Here are a few suggestions tailored to the Doctor's adventures:

- **Earl Grey:** Perfect for traditionalists who appreciate a classic pairing.
- **Chamomile:** A soothing option for unwinding after a long day of time travel.
- **Chai:** For a spicier, bolder experience, reminiscent of the exotic markets of Akhaten.

The Whovian Experience

Make your tea time a true *Doctor Who* event by serving these tea cakes with themed accompaniments. Set the table with a TARDIS teapot, Dalek-shaped sugar cubes, and napkins adorned with Gallifreyan script. Play the *Doctor Who* theme softly in the background, and let your imagination take you across the stars with every bite.

With their rich flavor, golden glaze, and celestial inspiration, these Gallifreyan Honey-Infused Tea Cakes are sure to become a favorite in your household—just as they might be for the Doctor. After all, no matter where you are in the universe, nothing beats the simple joy of tea and biscuits. Allons-y!

Chapter 2: TARDIS Blueberry Muffins

There's nothing quite as iconic in the *Doctor Who* universe as the TARDIS itself. Its deep, vibrant blue and endless mysteries inspire awe, nostalgia, and a sense of adventure. Translating this into a culinary masterpiece, we present TARDIS Blueberry Muffins—a delicious blend of classic comfort and intergalactic flair. Infused with a touch of Gallifreyan spices, these muffins are perfect for breakfast, tea time, or any moment you need a sweet treat to fuel your next adventure.

This chapter not only provides a recipe for these vibrant muffins but also explores creative ways to decorate them in true TARDIS fashion.

The Inspiration Behind TARDIS Blueberry Muffins

The TARDIS isn't just a time machine; it's a symbol of endless possibilities. These muffins, bursting with juicy blueberries and a hint of Gallifreyan spice, aim to capture that essence. Imagine sitting in the control room of the TARDIS with a warm muffin and a steaming cup of tea, ready to take on the next great journey.

Gallifreyan-Spiced Blueberry Muffins
Ingredients:
For the muffins:

- 2 cups all-purpose flour
- 2 tsp baking powder
- ½ tsp baking soda
- ¼ tsp salt
- ½ tsp ground cinnamon
- ¼ tsp ground cardamom
- ⅛ tsp ground star anise (optional for a cosmic twist)
- ½ cup unsalted butter, melted and cooled
- ¾ cup granulated sugar
- 2 large eggs
- 1 tsp vanilla extract
- ½ cup plain yogurt or sour cream
- ⅓ cup milk
- 1 ½ cups fresh or frozen blueberries

For the TARDIS glaze and decorations:

- 1 cup powdered sugar
- 2-3 tbsp milk or lemon juice
- Blue gel food coloring
- Edible silver stars or sprinkles
- White chocolate for creating TARDIS details

Instructions:
Step 1: Prepare the Muffin Batter

1. Preheat your oven to 375°F (190°C) and line a muffin tin with paper liners.
2. In a large bowl, whisk together the flour, baking powder, baking soda, salt, cinnamon, cardamom, and star anise. These spices bring a warm, slightly exotic flavor reminiscent of Gallifreyan sophistication.
3. In another bowl, whisk together the melted butter, sugar, eggs, and vanilla extract until smooth. Stir in the yogurt and milk until combined.
4. Gradually add the dry ingredients to the wet mixture, mixing just until combined. Be careful not to overmix to avoid dense muffins.
5. Gently fold in the blueberries, ensuring they are evenly distributed throughout the batter.

Step 2: Bake the Muffins

1. Divide the batter evenly among the muffin cups, filling each about ¾ full.
2. Bake for 20-25 minutes, or until the tops are golden brown and a toothpick inserted into the center comes out clean.
3. Let the muffins cool in the pan for 5 minutes before transferring them to a wire rack to cool completely.

Creating the TARDIS-Themed Glaze and Decorations

Now comes the fun part—turning these muffins into miniature edible TARDIS masterpieces!

Step 1: Make the TARDIS Glaze

1. In a small bowl, mix the powdered sugar with 2-3 tablespoons of milk or lemon juice to create a thick but pourable glaze.
2. Add a few drops of blue gel food coloring to achieve a deep TARDIS blue hue. Mix well.

Step 2: Glaze the Muffins

1. Once the muffins are completely cool, dip the tops into the blue glaze or spoon it over the tops. Allow the glaze to set slightly before adding decorations.

Step 3: Add the TARDIS Details

- **Edible Silver Stars:** Sprinkle edible silver stars or glitter over the glaze to mimic the starry backdrop of space.
- **White Chocolate TARDIS Panels:** Melt white chocolate and pipe or paint small TARDIS panel designs onto parchment paper. Once hardened, place these designs onto the tops of the muffins for a stunning TARDIS effect.

Optional: Use small edible paper sheets to create a "Police Public Call Box" label for extra authenticity.

Tips for Perfect TARDIS Blueberry Muffins

- **Prevent Sinking Blueberries:** Toss the blueberries in a tablespoon of flour before folding them into the batter. This helps prevent them from sinking to the bottom.
- **Adjust the Spice Level:** If you're not a fan of spices, feel free to reduce or omit the cardamom and star anise.
- **Enhance the Blueberry Flavor:** For an extra burst of blueberry flavor, mash ¼ cup of the blueberries and mix them into the batter before folding in the rest.

Serving Suggestions

- Pair these muffins with a cup of tea—Earl Grey, hot (as Captain Picard would say, though the Doctor might prefer something more adventurous).
- Serve them as part of a *Doctor Who*-themed tea party, complete with a TARDIS teapot and other space-inspired treats.
- For a festive twist, sprinkle the muffins with powdered sugar to mimic a snowy, wintery scene.

The Whovian Experience

These muffins are more than just a delicious treat—they're a celebration of the Doctor's enduring love for adventure, creativity, and connection. Every bite is a journey through flavor and imagination, making them a perfect addition to your holiday table or a *Doctor Who* viewing party.

So, gather your companions, set the table, and let these TARDIS Blueberry Muffins transport your taste buds through time and space. As the Doctor would say: "It's bigger on the inside!" Well, at least they'll taste like it is. Allons-y!

Chapter 3: Dalek Chocolate Truffles

Few villains in the *Doctor Who* universe are as iconic as the Daleks, with their distinctive design, metallic exteriors, and relentless pursuit of universal domination. What better way to pay homage to these infamous creatures than by turning them into something delectable? These Dalek Chocolate Truffles are as indulgent as they are fun, combining rich, creamy chocolate with customizable fillings.

Perfect for a *Doctor Who*-themed gathering or a holiday treat, these truffles allow you to exterminate boring desserts and create a conversation-starting centerpiece for your table.

The Concept: Edible Daleks

Daleks may be intimidating on screen, but in truffle form, they transform into delightful edible treats. This recipe blends creativity and culinary skill to recreate their iconic shape, complete with a variety of fillings to suit different tastes. From classic dark chocolate to refreshing mint and zesty orange, these truffles are sure to satisfy every palate.

Ingredients for Dalek Truffles

For the Chocolate Ganache Base:

- 10 oz (280 g) high-quality dark chocolate, finely chopped
- ½ cup heavy cream
- 2 tbsp unsalted butter, softened
- Pinch of salt

For the Variations:

- **Mint Filling:** 1 tsp peppermint extract + crushed mint candies for garnish
- **Orange Filling:** 1 tsp orange extract + zest of one orange
- **Dark Chocolate Filling:** 2 tbsp cocoa powder + 1 tbsp brewed espresso (optional)

For the Outer Coating:

- 8 oz (225 g) dark chocolate, melted for dipping
- 2 oz (50 g) white chocolate for piping details
- Edible metallic luster dust (optional, for a metallic Dalek finish)
- Sugar pearls or small candy balls for embellishments

Instructions: How to Make Dalek Truffles
Step 1: Prepare the Chocolate Ganache

1. Place the chopped dark chocolate in a heatproof bowl.
2. In a small saucepan, heat the heavy cream over medium heat until it just begins to simmer. Do not let it boil.
3. Pour the hot cream over the chopped chocolate and let it sit for 2-3 minutes to melt the chocolate.
4. Stir gently until smooth, then add the softened butter and a pinch of salt. Mix until fully combined.
5. If making a flavored variation, stir in the extract or other flavoring ingredients at this stage.

Step 2: Chill the Ganache

1. Cover the ganache with plastic wrap, pressing it directly onto the surface to prevent a skin from forming.
2. Refrigerate for 2-3 hours, or until the ganache is firm enough to shape.

Step 3: Shape the Dalek Truffles

1. Using a melon baller or small spoon, scoop out small portions of the ganache and roll them into balls for the Dalek body.
2. For the head, roll smaller balls and attach them to the body using a dab of melted chocolate.
3. Place the shaped truffles on a parchment-lined tray and freeze for 15-20 minutes to firm up.

Step 4: Decorate the Daleks

1. Melt the dark chocolate for dipping in a heatproof bowl over a pot of simmering water or in the microwave in 15-second intervals.
2. Using a fork or truffle dipper, coat each truffle in the melted chocolate and place it back on the tray.
3. Once the coating has set slightly, use a toothpick to add sugar pearls or small candy balls to create the Dalek's "bumps."
4. Melt the white chocolate and use a piping bag with a fine tip to add details like the Dalek's eyestalk, grilles, and other features.
5. For a metallic finish, lightly dust the truffles with edible luster dust once the chocolate is fully set.

Variations for Flavor Explorers
1. Mint Daleks:

- Add peppermint extract to the ganache for a refreshing flavor.
- Garnish with crushed mint candies or a green drizzle for a festive touch.

2. Orange Daleks:

- Stir in orange extract and zest for a zesty, citrusy twist.
- Add a candied orange peel segment to the top of each truffle for extra flair.

3. Dark Chocolate Espresso Daleks:

- Mix in cocoa powder and a splash of brewed espresso for a deep, rich flavor.
- Garnish with a sprinkle of cocoa powder or espresso powder for an elegant finish.

Tips for Perfect Dalek Truffles

- **Consistency Matters:** If the ganache is too soft to shape, return it to the fridge for additional chilling. If it's too hard, let it sit at room temperature for a few minutes.
- **Precision in Decoration:** Use tweezers to place the sugar pearls or candy balls for precise detailing.
- **Work in Batches:** Keep some ganache in the fridge while shaping to prevent it from becoming too soft.

Serving and Presentation

- Arrange the Dalek truffles on a serving tray lined with black or blue parchment paper for a dramatic presentation.
- For a *Doctor Who* theme, create a backdrop using a TARDIS model or printout.
- These truffles also make fantastic edible gifts when packaged in small boxes with *Doctor Who*-inspired designs.

The Whovian Experience

Dalek Chocolate Truffles aren't just a dessert; they're a testament to the power of creativity and fandom. Whether you're serving them at a holiday party, gifting them to a fellow *Doctor Who* fan, or simply treating yourself, these truffles are guaranteed to delight.

Remember, even the most menacing of foes can be transformed into something sweet and enjoyable with a little imagination. So, roll up your sleeves, prepare your ganache, and let these Dalek truffles "exterminate" any doubts about your culinary prowess!

As the Doctor might say, "Some people live more in twenty minutes of dessert-making than others do in twenty years. Be one of those people." Allons-y!

Chapter 4: Weeping Angel Wing Cookies

The Weeping Angels, some of the most terrifying and iconic villains in the *Doctor Who* universe, inspire this delicately delicious recipe. These sugar cookies, shaped like angel wings, transform the haunting elegance of the Angels into a treat that's perfect for themed parties, holidays, or simply indulging in a creative bake. With their intricate shapes and striking "stone" glaze, these cookies are as beautiful as they are tasty—just remember, **don't blink** while enjoying them!

The Concept: Edible Elegance Inspired by the Weeping Angels

The Weeping Angels are known for their eerie stillness and ancient stone-like appearance. In this recipe, that motif comes to life through intricate wing-shaped sugar cookies and a unique "stone" glaze effect. These cookies bring together simplicity and artistry, allowing even novice bakers to create a show-stopping treat.

Ingredients for Weeping Angel Wing Cookies

For the Sugar Cookie Base:

- 2 ½ cups all-purpose flour
- ½ tsp baking powder
- ¼ tsp salt
- ¾ cup unsalted butter, softened
- 1 cup granulated sugar
- 1 large egg
- 1 tsp vanilla extract
- ¼ tsp almond extract (optional, for added depth)

For the "Stone" Glaze:

- 1 ½ cups powdered sugar
- 2-3 tbsp milk or water
- ½ tsp vanilla extract (or almond extract for flavoring)
- Black gel food coloring
- White gel food coloring
- Edible silver luster dust (optional, for added shimmer)

Instructions: Crafting Weeping Angel Wing Cookies
Step 1: Prepare the Cookie Dough

1. In a medium bowl, whisk together the flour, baking powder, and salt. Set aside.
2. In a large mixing bowl, cream the softened butter and sugar together until light and fluffy, about 2-3 minutes.
3. Beat in the egg, vanilla extract, and almond extract (if using) until well combined.
4. Gradually add the dry ingredients to the wet mixture, mixing until a soft dough forms.
5. Divide the dough into two portions, wrap each in plastic wrap, and refrigerate for at least 1 hour. This ensures the dough is firm enough to roll and cut without losing shape.

Step 2: Cut and Bake the Wing Shapes

1. Preheat your oven to 350°F (175°C) and line baking sheets with parchment paper.
2. Roll out the chilled dough on a lightly floured surface to about ¼-inch thickness.
3. Use wing-shaped cookie cutters or create your own stencil from cardboard to cut out angel wing shapes. Transfer the cookies to the prepared baking sheets, spacing them about 1 inch apart.
4. Bake for 8-10 minutes, or until the edges are lightly golden. Be careful not to overbake, as the cookies should remain light in color to contrast with the glaze.
5. Allow the cookies to cool completely on a wire rack before decorating.

Step 3: Create the "Stone" Glaze
The glaze is where these cookies come to life, mimicking the texture and color of the Angels' stone appearance.

1. In a small bowl, whisk together the powdered sugar, milk or water, and vanilla extract until smooth. The glaze should be thick but pourable; adjust the consistency with more liquid or powdered sugar as needed.
2. Divide the glaze into three portions:
    ◦ One portion will remain white.
    ◦ One portion will be tinted gray using black gel food coloring.
    ◦ One portion will be tinted a slightly darker gray with additional black food coloring.
3. Use a small spoon or piping bag to coat each cookie with a base layer of light gray glaze. Let this layer dry for 10-15 minutes.

Step 4: Add the Stone Effect

1. Once the base layer is set but not fully hardened, use a small, clean brush or a toothpick to dab the darker gray glaze onto the surface. Create a mottled, uneven pattern to mimic the texture of stone.
2. Use the white glaze sparingly to highlight certain areas of the wings, such as edges or feather details.
3. For added realism, lightly dust the cookies with edible silver luster dust once the glaze is fully dry. This gives the wings a subtle shimmer, reminiscent of aged stone.

Tips for Perfect Angel Wing Cookies

- **Shape Precision:** If you don't have a wing-shaped cutter, print out an angel wing design, cut it out, and use it as a stencil to trace the shape onto your dough with a sharp knife.
- **Chill Time:** Ensure the dough is well-chilled before rolling it out to prevent spreading during baking.
- **Layered Glaze:** Apply the glaze in thin layers, allowing each to dry slightly before adding the next. This helps create depth and texture.
- **Practice Makes Perfect:** If you're new to glazing cookies, practice your "stone effect" technique on a piece of parchment paper before applying it to the cookies.

Serving and Presentation Ideas

- **Display Elegance:** Arrange the cookies on a dark platter or slate board for a dramatic presentation that evokes the Angels' gothic aesthetic.
- **Gift-Worthy:** Package the cookies in clear cellophane bags tied with gray or silver ribbon for a stunning edible gift.
- **Themed Party Highlight:** Pair these cookies with other *Doctor Who*-inspired treats, like TARDIS Blueberry Muffins or Dalek Chocolate Truffles, for a cohesive Whovian dessert spread.

The Whovian Experience

The Weeping Angels might be terrifying, but these cookies are anything but. They combine the elegance of angel wings with the gritty texture of stone, making them a unique addition to your *Doctor Who* culinary adventure.

Whether you're serving these at a holiday gathering, a themed party, or simply enjoying them with a cup of tea, these cookies are a testament to the creativity and fun of fandom-inspired baking. So, go ahead, bake these angelic treats—and remember, **don't blink** while decorating. You never know what might happen when you look away.

Allons-y!

Chapter 5: Cybermen Cyber-Cookies

The Cybermen, with their sleek metallic exteriors and cold efficiency, are some of the most recognizable foes in the *Doctor Who* universe. In this chapter, we bring their futuristic aesthetic to life with Cybermen Cyber-Cookies—delicate, buttery shortbread cookies with a metallic silver twist. These cookies are simple to make but pack a visual punch, combining the classic appeal of shortbread with an elegant, futuristic glaze enhanced with edible glitter for that unmistakable Cyberman shine.

The Inspiration: A Cookie Fit for the Cybermen

The Cybermen represent the fusion of humanity and machine, their metallic forms reflecting a vision of streamlined efficiency and power. These cookies take cues from their design with a metallic silver glaze and precise, geometric shapes. Whether you're hosting a *Doctor Who*-themed party or just looking for a standout dessert, Cybermen Cyber-Cookies are sure to impress.

Ingredients for Cyber-Cookies

For the Shortbread Base:

- 1 cup unsalted butter, softened
- ½ cup granulated sugar
- 1 tsp vanilla extract
- 2 cups all-purpose flour
- ¼ tsp salt

For the Metallic Glaze:

- 1 ½ cups powdered sugar
- 2-3 tbsp milk or water
- 1 tsp vanilla extract or almond extract
- Silver gel food coloring
- Edible silver glitter or luster dust

Optional Decorations:

- Black gel food coloring for Cyberman details
- Small round edible pearls or candies for "cybernetic" embellishments

Instructions: Crafting Cybermen Cyber-Cookies
Step 1: Prepare the Shortbread Dough

1. In a large mixing bowl, cream together the softened butter and sugar until light and fluffy, about 2-3 minutes.
2. Mix in the vanilla extract until combined.
3. Gradually add the flour and salt, mixing until the dough comes together. It should be soft but not sticky.
4. Divide the dough into two portions, wrap each in plastic wrap, and refrigerate for at least 1 hour. This helps the dough hold its shape during baking.

Step 2: Shape and Bake the Cookies

1. Preheat your oven to 325°F (160°C) and line baking sheets with parchment paper.
2. Roll out the chilled dough on a lightly floured surface to about ¼-inch thickness.
3. Use Cyberman-shaped cookie cutters, or opt for simple geometric shapes like circles, rectangles, or hexagons to reflect their sleek, futuristic style.
4. Transfer the cookies to the prepared baking sheets, spacing them about 1 inch apart.
5. Bake for 12-15 minutes, or until the edges are just lightly golden. Do not overbake, as shortbread should remain pale.
6. Allow the cookies to cool completely on a wire rack before decorating.

Step 3: Create the Metallic Glaze
The glaze is key to achieving the Cybermen's signature metallic look.

1. In a small bowl, whisk together the powdered sugar, milk or water, and vanilla extract until smooth and glossy. The glaze should be thick enough to coat the cookies but still spreadable; adjust consistency with more liquid or sugar as needed.
2. Add a few drops of silver gel food coloring and mix well until the glaze has a uniform metallic sheen.

Step 4: Glaze the Cookies

1. Using a spoon or small offset spatula, spread the silver glaze evenly over the tops of the cooled cookies.
2. While the glaze is still wet, sprinkle edible silver glitter or luster dust over the cookies for a sparkling, futuristic finish.

Step 5: Add Cyberman Details (Optional)

1. To create Cyberman faces or designs, mix a small portion of the glaze with black gel food coloring.
2. Use a fine-tipped piping bag or a toothpick to draw features like the iconic Cyberman "handles" or other cybernetic patterns.
3. For added dimension, attach small edible pearls or candies to mimic the Cybermen's mechanical components.

Tips for Perfect Cyber-Cookies

- **Keep It Cool:** Chilled dough holds its shape better, so if the dough softens while working, return it to the fridge for 10-15 minutes before continuing.
- **Sharp Edges:** Use sharp cookie cutters or a precision knife for clean, geometric shapes.
- **Glaze Drying Time:** Allow the glaze to set completely (about 1-2 hours) before stacking or storing the cookies.
- **Experiment with Shapes:** If you don't have Cyberman-shaped cutters, use hexagons, squares, or circles to evoke their futuristic aesthetic.

Serving and Presentation Ideas

- **Futuristic Display:** Serve the cookies on a mirrored platter or a sleek, metallic tray to highlight their shiny glaze.
- **Themed Pairings:** Pair these Cyber-Cookies with TARDIS Blueberry Muffins or Dalek Chocolate Truffles for a full *Doctor Who* dessert spread.
- **Giftable Treats:** Package the cookies in silver boxes or tins with a Cyberman motif for a unique edible gift.

The Whovian Experience

These Cybermen Cyber-Cookies blend the timeless appeal of buttery shortbread with a futuristic design that celebrates one of *Doctor Who*'s most iconic villains. The combination of rich, crumbly texture and eye-catching metallic glaze makes these cookies a standout treat for any occasion.

Just like the Cybermen themselves, these cookies are a testament to precision and efficiency—but unlike their on-screen counterparts, they're guaranteed to bring joy rather than terror to anyone who encounters them. So, get your baking gear ready and let these cookies "upgrade" your dessert game.

And remember: Resistance to these cookies is futile. Allons-y!

Chapter 6: Sonic Screwdriver Spritzers

The Sonic Screwdriver is more than just a tool—it's an iconic symbol of the Doctor's ingenuity, resourcefulness, and a touch of whimsy. What better way to celebrate its legacy than with a festive drink inspired by its vibrant colors and versatile nature? Sonic Screwdriver Spritzers are a delightful addition to any holiday or *Doctor Who*-themed gathering, offering both non-alcoholic and adult-friendly options to suit every guest's preference.

In this chapter, we'll explore how to create these dazzling spritzers, with layers of flavor and a sparkling presentation that mirrors the magic of the Doctor's most indispensable gadget.

The Concept: A Drink Worthy of the Sonic Screwdriver

Like the tool it's named after, the Sonic Screwdriver Spritzer is versatile, refreshing, and always ready to impress. These drinks combine the effervescence of sparkling water or soda with vibrant juices and creative garnishes to create a visually stunning beverage. The non-alcoholic version ensures everyone can join in the fun, while the adult-friendly variations add an extra layer of sophistication with spirits like vodka, gin, or prosecco.

Ingredients for Sonic Screwdriver Spritzers
Non-Alcoholic Version:

- 1 cup orange juice (freshly squeezed if possible)
- ½ cup pineapple juice
- 1 tbsp grenadine
- 1 cup sparkling water, lemon-lime soda, or ginger ale
- Ice cubes
- Blue curaçao syrup (non-alcoholic) for color
- Lemon or orange slices for garnish
- Edible glitter (optional, for a sparkling effect)

Adult-Friendly Version:

- 1 cup orange juice
- ½ cup pineapple juice
- 1 tbsp grenadine
- 1 cup prosecco, sparkling wine, or club soda (for a lighter version)
- 1-2 oz vodka or gin
- Ice cubes
- Blue curaçao liqueur for color
- Citrus slices and sprigs of mint for garnish

Instructions: Crafting Sonic Screwdriver Spritzers
Step 1: Prepare the Base

1. In a large pitcher, combine the orange juice, pineapple juice, and grenadine. Stir gently to mix.
2. Taste the mixture and adjust the sweetness or tartness as needed by adding a splash of lemon juice or a drizzle of honey.

Step 2: Layer the Drink

1. Fill each glass with ice cubes.
2. Pour the juice mixture into the glass, filling it about two-thirds full.
3. For the vibrant Sonic Screwdriver effect, slowly pour the sparkling water, soda, or prosecco over the back of a spoon into the glass. This technique helps create a layered look.

Step 3: Add the Sonic Touch

1. For the iconic blue color, drizzle a small amount of blue curaçao syrup (non-alcoholic) or liqueur into the drink. It will sink to the bottom, creating a gradient effect reminiscent of the Sonic Screwdriver's glow.
2. Gently stir the drink with a straw to incorporate the colors while maintaining the layered appearance.

Step 4: Garnish and Serve

1. Add a slice of lemon or orange to the rim of the glass for a bright, festive touch.
2. Sprinkle a pinch of edible glitter over the top for a sparkling, otherworldly effect.
3. For the adult version, garnish with a sprig of mint or a skewer of fresh fruit for added sophistication.

Variations for the Perfect Spritzer

1. Tropical Sonic Screwdriver:

- Replace the pineapple juice with mango or passionfruit juice for a tropical twist.
- Add coconut water for a hydrating, beach-inspired version.

2. Berry-Infused Screwdriver:

- Substitute grenadine with raspberry or strawberry syrup for a berry-forward flavor.
- Muddle fresh berries at the bottom of the glass for added texture and visual appeal.

3. Holiday Sonic Screwdriver:

- Incorporate cranberry juice instead of pineapple juice for a festive red hue.
- Garnish with sugared cranberries and a sprig of rosemary for a winter wonderland effect.

4. Galactic Sparkle Screwdriver:

- Add a drop of edible color-changing powder for a magical, interactive drink.
- Use sparkling lemonade for a tangy twist.

Tips for Crafting the Perfect Sonic Screwdriver Spritzer

- **Layering Mastery:** Use a spoon to layer liquids with different densities, pouring gently to create a gradient effect.
- **Chill Ingredients:** Ensure all juices, sodas, and spirits are well-chilled before mixing to maintain the spritzer's refreshing quality.
- **Garnish Creativity:** Play with creative garnishes like star-shaped fruit slices or glow-in-the-dark cocktail stirrers to elevate the theme.
- **Batch Preparation:** For large gatherings, prepare the juice mixture in advance and add the sparkling components just before serving to preserve effervescence.

Serving and Presentation Ideas

- **TARDIS Touch:** Serve the spritzers in blue-tinted glasses or use light-up LED ice cubes for a futuristic vibe.
- **Party Centerpiece:** Arrange the glasses on a tray surrounded by string lights or small *Doctor Who* figurines for a themed display.
- **Personalized Options:** Create a "build-your-own spritzer" station with a selection of juices, syrups, and garnishes so guests can customize their drinks.

The Whovian Experience

The Sonic Screwdriver Spritzers are more than just drinks—they're an invitation to celebrate the creativity, energy, and fun of *Doctor Who*. Whether you're sipping a non-alcoholic version with family or raising a glass of the adult-friendly variety with friends, these spritzers capture the spirit of adventure and innovation that the Doctor embodies.

So, grab your glasses, toast to the wonders of the universe, and let these sparkling beverages light up your festivities—no actual Sonic Screwdriver required (but highly encouraged for decoration). **Geronimo!**

Chapter 7: Gallifreyan Gingerbread Villages

Few locations in the *Doctor Who* universe are as evocative and mysterious as Gallifrey, the home planet of the Time Lords. Imagine recreating the majestic spires, domes, and golden glow of Gallifrey in edible form. In this chapter, we'll take you on a culinary adventure to build your very own gingerbread Gallifrey, complete with a recipe for sturdy and flavorful gingerbread, royal icing for construction, and creative ideas for edible decorations.

The Inspiration: A Taste of Gallifrey

Gallifrey's skyline, dominated by towering citadels, intricate domes, and the iconic orange skies, offers a perfect blueprint for a show-stopping gingerbread display. This project is not only a delicious holiday treat but also an opportunity to flex your creativity and immerse yourself in the *Doctor Who* universe. Whether you're making a small village or an elaborate gingerbread city, this guide will ensure your Gallifreyan masterpiece is out of this world.

Ingredients for Gallifreyan Gingerbread Villages

For the Gingerbread Dough:

- 3 ¼ cups all-purpose flour
- 1 tsp baking soda
- ½ tsp salt
- 2 tsp ground ginger
- 1 tsp ground cinnamon
- ½ tsp ground cloves
- ½ cup unsalted butter, softened
- ½ cup granulated sugar
- ½ cup molasses
- 1 large egg
- 1 tsp vanilla extract

For the Royal Icing (Construction and Decoration):

- 3 large egg whites (or 6 tbsp pasteurized egg whites for safety)
- 4 cups powdered sugar, sifted
- 1 tsp lemon juice or vanilla extract

For Edible Decorations:

- Gel food coloring (gold, red, and orange for Gallifreyan themes)
- Edible metallic luster dust (gold and silver)
- Small round candies or sugar pearls for domes and spires
- Chocolate sticks or pretzels for architectural details
- Shredded coconut tinted with food coloring for "landscaping"
- Edible glitter for a cosmic touch

Instructions: Crafting Your Gingerbread Gallifrey
Step 1: Prepare the Gingerbread Dough

1. In a medium bowl, whisk together the flour, baking soda, salt, ginger, cinnamon, and cloves. Set aside.
2. In a large mixing bowl, cream the softened butter and sugar until light and fluffy, about 2-3 minutes.
3. Mix in the molasses, egg, and vanilla extract until fully combined.
4. Gradually add the dry ingredients to the wet mixture, mixing until a firm dough forms.
5. Divide the dough into two portions, wrap each in plastic wrap, and refrigerate for at least 1 hour (or up to overnight).

Step 2: Cut and Bake the Gingerbread Pieces

1. Preheat your oven to 350°F (175°C) and line baking sheets with parchment paper.
2. Roll out the chilled dough on a lightly floured surface to about ¼-inch thickness.
3. Use stencils or freehand designs to cut out pieces for your Gallifreyan structures, such as circular domes, triangular spires, and rectangular walls. For added flair, create window cutouts or use small cutters to imprint designs.
4. Transfer the pieces to the prepared baking sheets and bake for 10-12 minutes, or until the edges are firm and slightly darkened.
5. Allow the pieces to cool completely on a wire rack before assembly.

Step 3: Make the Royal Icing

1. In a large mixing bowl, beat the egg whites and lemon juice until frothy.
2. Gradually add the powdered sugar, mixing on low speed until the icing reaches a thick, pipeable consistency.
3. Divide the icing into portions and color as desired using gel food coloring. Keep the icing covered with a damp cloth when not in use to prevent it from drying out.

Step 4: Assemble the Gallifreyan Structures

1. Use royal icing as "mortar" to glue the gingerbread pieces together. Start with the base walls and allow them to set before adding domes, spires, or other architectural features.
2. For domes, use rounded molds (like bowls or hemispherical pans) to shape gingerbread pieces before baking, or construct domes by cutting pieces into curved shapes and gluing them together with icing.
3. Allow the assembled structures to dry completely before decorating.

Step 5: Decorate Your Gingerbread Gallifrey

1. **Metallic Domes and Spires:** Paint edible gold or silver luster dust mixed with a small amount of vodka or lemon extract onto domes and spires for a radiant Gallifreyan glow.
2. **Cosmic Accents:** Use edible glitter or shimmer powders to mimic the starry backdrop of Gallifrey's skies.
3. **Candy Embellishments:** Attach sugar pearls or round candies to mimic futuristic details and ornamentation.
4. **Landscaping:** Use shredded coconut tinted with green food coloring to create alien flora around your structures. Add small candies or colored sugar for vibrant, otherworldly accents.
5. **Gallifreyan Symbols:** Pipe intricate designs onto walls or bases using colored royal icing to mimic the Gallifreyan script.

Tips for a Stunning Gingerbread Gallifrey

- **Plan Ahead:** Sketch your designs and create stencils for more precise gingerbread pieces.
- **Reinforce Larger Structures:** For added stability, use melted sugar or caramel as a strong adhesive in addition to royal icing.
- **Use a Lazy Susan:** If you're working on a larger, circular design, a rotating base makes decorating easier.
- **Details Matter:** Small embellishments like edible glitter and luster dust elevate the look of your village, making it feel more authentic to Gallifreyan lore.

Serving and Presentation Ideas

- **Themed Display:** Place your gingerbread Gallifrey on a mirrored tray to reflect its intricate details and enhance the "golden glow."
- **Interactive Dessert:** Encourage guests to break off pieces of the gingerbread village to enjoy during your gathering.
- **Photo-Worthy Centerpiece:** This edible village doubles as a holiday centerpiece, perfect for photos and Instagram-worthy moments.

The Whovian Experience

Building your own gingerbread Gallifrey is more than just a baking project—it's a creative journey into the heart of the *Doctor Who* universe. Each structure you craft pays homage to the timeless elegance and mystery of the Time Lords' home planet.

So, gather your ingredients, unleash your inner architect, and create a gingerbread masterpiece that's as delicious as it is impressive. Whether you're celebrating the holidays, hosting a *Doctor Who* party, or simply indulging your fandom, this edible Gallifrey is sure to leave everyone in awe.

As the Doctor might say: "Timey-wimey… tasty-wasty!" Allons-y!

Chapter 8: The Timey-Wimey Pudding

Sticky toffee pudding is a classic dessert with its rich, moist sponge and decadent caramel sauce, but this version takes it to a whole new level. Inspired by the Doctor's famous "timey-wimey" quip, the Timey-Wimey Pudding features a unique caramel core that creates the illusion of a time loop as it oozes out with every slice. And to make it even more theatrical, we'll show you how to serve it with flaming brandy for a dazzling presentation that's perfect for holidays or *Doctor Who* celebrations.

The Concept: A Time Loop of Flavor

Sticky toffee pudding is already a crowd-pleaser, but the Timey-Wimey Pudding adds a twist. The caramel core is baked right into the center, creating a surprise that flows like a time vortex when you cut into the dessert. The flaming brandy not only adds drama but also deepens the caramelized flavors, making this dish as unforgettable as the Doctor's greatest adventures.

Ingredients for the Timey-Wimey Pudding

For the Pudding Base:

- 1 ½ cups dates, pitted and chopped
- 1 ¼ cups boiling water
- 1 tsp baking soda
- ½ cup unsalted butter, softened
- ¾ cup brown sugar
- 2 large eggs
- 1 ½ cups all-purpose flour
- 1 tsp baking powder
- 1 tsp vanilla extract
- ½ tsp ground cinnamon

For the Caramel "Time Loop" Core:

- 1 cup granulated sugar
- ¼ cup water
- ½ cup heavy cream
- 2 tbsp unsalted butter
- Pinch of salt

For the Flaming Brandy Sauce:

- ½ cup brandy or rum
- ½ cup caramel sauce (reserved from the core recipe)

Instructions: Creating the Timey-Wimey Pudding
Step 1: Prepare the Sticky Toffee Pudding Batter

1. Preheat your oven to 350°F (175°C) and grease a deep 8-inch round cake pan or pudding mold.
2. Place the chopped dates in a bowl and pour the boiling water over them. Stir in the baking soda and let the mixture sit for 10 minutes to soften. Mash lightly with a fork to create a coarse paste.
3. In a large mixing bowl, cream together the butter and brown sugar until light and fluffy.
4. Add the eggs one at a time, beating well after each addition. Stir in the vanilla extract.
5. In a separate bowl, whisk together the flour, baking powder, and cinnamon. Gradually fold the dry ingredients into the wet mixture.
6. Finally, mix in the date paste until fully incorporated.

Step 2: Create the Caramel "Time Loop" Core

1. In a medium saucepan, combine the sugar and water over medium heat. Stir gently until the sugar dissolves, then stop stirring and allow the mixture to boil until it turns a deep amber color.
2. Carefully whisk in the heavy cream (the mixture will bubble up), then add the butter and a pinch of salt. Stir until smooth.
3. Reserve ½ cup of the caramel for the flaming brandy sauce and set it aside. Allow the remaining caramel to cool slightly before use.

Step 3: Assemble and Bake

1. Pour half of the pudding batter into the prepared pan.
2. Spoon the caramel into the center of the batter, leaving a small border around the edges to prevent leaking.
3. Cover with the remaining batter, ensuring the caramel is fully encased.
4. Bake for 45-50 minutes, or until a skewer inserted near the edge of the pudding comes out clean (avoid the center, as the caramel core will remain molten).

Step 4: Prepare the Flaming Brandy Sauce

1. In a small saucepan, combine the reserved caramel sauce with the brandy or rum. Heat gently over low heat until warmed through.
2. Just before serving, transfer the sauce to a heatproof ladle or small saucepan for flaming.

Step 5: Serve with Flaming Brandy

1. Carefully warm the ladle or saucepan of brandy sauce over a low flame or stove burner until it begins to produce vapors (but avoid letting it boil).
2. Dim the lights for dramatic effect. Using a long lighter or match, ignite the sauce and pour the flaming mixture over the pudding.
3. Allow the flames to subside before slicing the pudding and serving.

Tips for a Perfect Timey-Wimey Pudding

- **Seal the Caramel Core:** Ensure the caramel is fully encased by the batter to prevent leaks during baking.
- **Caramel Mastery:** Watch the caramel closely as it cooks to avoid burning. If it darkens too quickly, reduce the heat slightly.
- **Safety First:** When flaming the brandy, keep a fire extinguisher or damp towel nearby for safety, and always pour the flaming sauce away from guests.
- **Presentation:** Serve slices with a drizzle of extra caramel sauce and a dollop of whipped cream or a scoop of vanilla ice cream for added indulgence.

Serving and Presentation Ideas

- **TARDIS Flair:** Place the pudding on a blue serving plate to evoke the Doctor's time machine.
- **Themed Garnishes:** Decorate the plate with edible gold stars or sprinkles to mimic the time vortex.
- **Interactive Dessert:** Encourage guests to slice into the pudding and watch the caramel core flow like a time loop, creating a fun and surprising moment.

The Whovian Experience

The Timey-Wimey Pudding is a dessert that embodies the magic, mystery, and theatrical flair of *Doctor Who*. Its sticky toffee base and molten caramel core make it a rich and satisfying treat, while the flaming brandy adds a dramatic touch that's sure to leave a lasting impression.

So, gather your companions, dim the lights, and let this pudding transport your taste buds through time and space. As the Doctor might say, "People assume that dessert is a strict progression of pudding to sauce... but actually, from a non-linear, non-subjective viewpoint, it's more like a big, sticky, caramel ball of yumminess."

Allons-y!

Chapter 9: Ood-Approved Spiced Eggnog

The Ood, those serene and thoughtful creatures from the *Doctor Who* universe, are known for their wisdom, grace, and understated charm. What better way to pay homage to these gentle beings than with a rich, spiced eggnog that's just as comforting as their calming presence? Ood-Approved Spiced Eggnog combines classic holiday flavors with an intergalactic twist, making it the perfect drink for any festive occasion.

This recipe is fully customizable, offering options for vegan and lactose-free variations, so everyone at your gathering can enjoy its "Ood-ly" delicious flavors.

The Inspiration: A Comforting Sip of the Universe

Eggnog, with its creamy texture and warm spices, is a quintessential holiday beverage. This version takes it a step further with the addition of unique spices and subtle citrus notes, evoking the mysterious yet harmonious nature of the Ood. Whether served hot or chilled, this eggnog will transport you to the tranquil realms of the Ood Sphere.

Ingredients for Ood-Approved Spiced Eggnog
Traditional Eggnog Base:

- 4 large egg yolks
- ½ cup granulated sugar
- 2 cups whole milk
- 1 cup heavy cream
- ½ tsp ground cinnamon
- ¼ tsp ground nutmeg (plus extra for garnish)
- ¼ tsp ground cardamom (optional, for a cosmic twist)
- 1 tsp vanilla extract
- Zest of 1 orange (optional, for a subtle citrus note)
- ½ cup rum, bourbon, or brandy (optional, for an adult-friendly version)

Vegan and Lactose-Free Version:

- 2 cups unsweetened almond milk, oat milk, or coconut milk
- 1 cup coconut cream or cashew cream
- 4 tbsp maple syrup or agave nectar (as a sugar substitute)
- ½ tsp ground cinnamon
- ¼ tsp ground nutmeg (plus extra for garnish)
- ¼ tsp ground cardamom
- 1 tsp vanilla extract
- Zest of 1 orange (optional)
- ½ cup rum, bourbon, or brandy (optional, for an adult-friendly version)

Instructions: Crafting Ood-Approved Spiced Eggnog
Step 1: Prepare the Eggnog Base

1. In a medium bowl, whisk the egg yolks with the sugar until the mixture is pale and slightly thickened. (For the vegan version, skip this step and proceed to the next.)
2. In a saucepan over medium heat, combine the milk, cream, cinnamon, nutmeg, cardamom, and orange zest. Heat until the mixture is warm but not boiling.
3. Gradually whisk about ½ cup of the warm milk mixture into the egg yolks to temper them, then slowly pour the tempered egg mixture back into the saucepan while whisking continuously.
4. Cook the mixture over low heat, stirring constantly, until it thickens slightly and coats the back of a spoon (about 5-7 minutes). Do not let it boil.
5. For the vegan version, heat the plant-based milk, cream, and spices in the same way, stirring in the maple syrup or agave nectar until dissolved.

Step 2: Add Flavorings and Chill

1. Remove the saucepan from heat and stir in the vanilla extract. If you're adding alcohol, stir it in at this stage.
2. Pour the eggnog through a fine mesh sieve into a large bowl or pitcher to remove any solids and ensure a smooth texture.
3. Cover and refrigerate for at least 2 hours, or until thoroughly chilled.

Step 3: Serve with Ood-Like Elegance

1. Pour the chilled eggnog into glasses or mugs, and garnish with a sprinkle of nutmeg or a cinnamon stick.
2. For a festive touch, add whipped cream (or coconut whipped cream for vegan/lactose-free) and a light dusting of edible glitter to evoke the celestial qualities of the Ood Sphere.

Tips for Perfect Ood-Approved Eggnog

- **Safety First:** If you're concerned about raw eggs, use pasteurized egg yolks or gently cook the egg mixture until it reaches 160°F (71°C).
- **Spice Balance:** Adjust the spice levels to suit your taste, adding more cinnamon or nutmeg for a bolder flavor.
- **Citrus Note:** The orange zest adds a bright, unique twist to the traditional eggnog flavor, but it's optional if you prefer a more classic taste.
- **Make It Frothy:** For a lighter texture, whisk or blend the chilled eggnog before serving.

Serving and Presentation Ideas

- **Ood-Inspired Garnishes:** Use cinnamon sticks or stirrers shaped like the Ood's translator globes to tie the theme together.
- **Themed Glassware:** Serve the eggnog in clear glasses or mugs to highlight its creamy color and festive garnishes.
- **Chilled or Warm:** While traditionally served cold, this eggnog can also be gently warmed for a cozy, wintery drink.

Customizations and Variations
1. Chocolate Ood Eggnog:

- Add 2 tbsp cocoa powder to the base mixture for a rich, chocolatey twist.
- Garnish with chocolate shavings or a drizzle of chocolate syrup.

2. Spiked Ood Delight:

- Experiment with different spirits, such as amaretto or spiced rum, for unique flavor profiles.

3. Galactic Swirl Eggnog:

- Stir in a few drops of edible glitter or luster dust before serving to create a shimmering, cosmic effect.

4. Coffee-Infused Eggnog:

- Replace ½ cup of the milk with strong brewed coffee or espresso for a caffeinated twist.

The Whovian Experience
Ood-Approved Spiced Eggnog is more than a holiday drink—it's a celebration of connection, kindness, and the warmth of shared moments. With its rich, spiced flavors and customizable options, this eggnog is sure to bring people together, much like the Ood themselves.

So, raise your glass and toast to the wonders of the universe, the brilliance of the Doctor, and the gentle wisdom of the Ood. "The circle must be broken"—but in this case, it's a circle of friends around the table, enjoying this "Ood-ly" delicious creation.
Allons-y!

Chapter 10: Rassilon's Regal Roast

Rassilon, the legendary founder of Time Lord society, is synonymous with grandeur, power, and legacy. What better way to pay tribute to such a figure than with a majestic roast fit for the high council of Gallifrey? Rassilon's Regal Roast is a show-stopping main dish inspired by Gallifreyan elegance, complemented by uniquely flavored sides: "Temporal Taters" and "Galaxy Greens." This feast is designed to transport your guests to the dining halls of the Time Lords, blending earthly ingredients with cosmic creativity.

The Inspiration: A Feast Fit for the Lords of Time

Gallifreyan cuisine, while largely mysterious, can be imagined as sophisticated, aromatic, and infused with a touch of otherworldly creativity. Rassilon's Regal Roast embodies this spirit with a perfectly seasoned main dish, enhanced by sides that incorporate unique flavor profiles inspired by the endless possibilities of time and space.

Ingredients for Rassilon's Regal Roast

For the Roast (Serves 6-8):

- 4-5 lb beef tenderloin, leg of lamb, or whole chicken (your choice of protein)
- 2 tbsp olive oil
- 4 cloves garlic, minced
- 2 tbsp fresh rosemary, finely chopped
- 1 tbsp fresh thyme leaves
- 1 tsp ground coriander
- 1 tsp smoked paprika
- 1 tsp salt
- ½ tsp black pepper
- Zest of 1 lemon (optional, for brightness)

For the Temporal Taters (Roasted Potatoes):

- 2 lbs baby potatoes, halved
- 3 tbsp olive oil
- 1 tsp ground turmeric
- 1 tsp smoked paprika
- 1 tsp garlic powder
- ½ tsp salt
- ¼ tsp black pepper
- 1 tbsp fresh parsley, chopped (for garnish)

For the Galaxy Greens (Sautéed Vegetables):

- 1 lb broccolini or green beans
- 1 cup sugar snap peas
- 1 tbsp olive oil or butter
- 2 cloves garlic, minced
- 1 tsp ground ginger
- 1 tsp sesame oil (optional, for an earthy flavor)
- 1 tbsp soy sauce or tamari (for a gluten-free option)
- 1 tbsp sesame seeds (for garnish)

Instructions: Crafting Rassilon's Regal Roast
Step 1: Prepare the Roast

1. Preheat your oven to 375°F (190°C).
2. Pat the roast dry with paper towels and place it on a roasting rack inside a baking dish.
3. In a small bowl, mix the olive oil, garlic, rosemary, thyme, coriander, smoked paprika, salt, black pepper, and lemon zest (if using).
4. Rub the herb mixture all over the roast, ensuring even coverage. For added flavor, let the roast marinate for 30 minutes to 1 hour at room temperature or overnight in the refrigerator.

Step 2: Cook the Roast

1. Roast the meat in the preheated oven until it reaches your desired level of doneness:
    - Beef: 130°F (54°C) for medium-rare, 140°F (60°C) for medium.
    - Lamb: 135°F (57°C) for medium-rare, 145°F (63°C) for medium.
    - Chicken: 165°F (74°C) for fully cooked.
2. Use a meat thermometer to ensure accuracy, checking the internal temperature in the thickest part of the meat.
3. Once cooked, remove the roast from the oven and let it rest for 10-15 minutes before slicing.

Instructions: Temporal Taters (Roasted Potatoes)
Step 1: Prepare the Potatoes

1. Preheat your oven to 400°F (200°C).
2. In a large bowl, toss the halved baby potatoes with olive oil, turmeric, smoked paprika, garlic powder, salt, and black pepper until evenly coated.

Step 2: Roast the Potatoes

1. Spread the potatoes in a single layer on a baking sheet lined with parchment paper.
2. Roast in the preheated oven for 25-30 minutes, flipping halfway through, until golden brown and crispy on the edges.
3. Garnish with fresh parsley before serving.

Instructions: Galaxy Greens (Sautéed Vegetables)
Step 1: Prepare the Vegetables

1. Trim the ends of the broccolini or green beans and rinse the sugar snap peas. Pat dry.

Step 2: Sauté the Vegetables

1. Heat olive oil or butter in a large skillet over medium heat. Add the minced garlic and ground ginger, cooking until fragrant (about 1 minute).
2. Add the broccolini or green beans and cook for 3-4 minutes, stirring occasionally.
3. Add the sugar snap peas and cook for an additional 2-3 minutes, until the vegetables are tender-crisp.
4. Stir in the sesame oil and soy sauce, mixing to coat the vegetables evenly.

Step 3: Garnish and Serve

1. Sprinkle sesame seeds over the vegetables just before serving for a touch of elegance.

Plating and Presentation

- Arrange the sliced roast on a large platter, surrounded by the Temporal Taters and Galaxy Greens for a cohesive presentation.
- Drizzle the roast with its pan juices or a simple gravy for added richness.
- For a Gallifreyan aesthetic, garnish the platter with sprigs of fresh herbs and edible flowers to mimic the elegance of the Time Lords' feasts.

Tips for a Perfect Gallifreyan-Inspired Feast

- **Even Cooking:** Allow the roast to come to room temperature before cooking for more even heat distribution.
- **Crispy Potatoes:** To ensure crispy roasted potatoes, pat them dry before tossing them in oil and spices.
- **Balanced Greens:** Don't overcook the vegetables—retain their vibrant color and slight crunch to keep them "fresh from the galaxy."

The Whovian Experience

Rassilon's Regal Roast, with its perfectly seasoned meat, golden potatoes, and vibrant vegetables, is a feast that captures the essence of Gallifreyan sophistication. Whether you're hosting a holiday gathering or a *Doctor Who*-themed dinner, this dish is sure to impress.

As you slice into the tender roast and savor the harmonious blend of flavors, you'll feel as though you've been transported to the grand halls of the Time Lords. Raise a glass, toast to the wonders of time and space, and enjoy this culinary masterpiece worthy of Rassilon himself.

Allons-y!

Chapter 11: Slitheen Sliders

The Slitheen, with their mischievous personalities and signature green hues, are unforgettable creatures from the *Doctor Who* universe. In this chapter, we channel their playful spirit into a dish that's equally fun and delicious: Slitheen Sliders! These bite-sized burgers, customizable with meat or vegetarian patties, are topped with creative, alien-inspired ingredients to bring a taste of Raxacoricofallapatorius to your table. Perfect for parties, themed events, or family dinners, these sliders will have everyone exclaiming, "Fantastic!"

The Concept: Playful and Alien-Inspired Burgers

Slitheen Sliders are all about creativity and adaptability. Their small size makes them perfect for experimenting with toppings, sauces, and presentations. Inspired by the Slitheen's green color and unusual features, these sliders incorporate vibrant greens, unique flavor combinations, and a playful presentation that's out of this world.

Ingredients for Slitheen Sliders
For the Meat Patties (Makes 12 sliders):

- 1 lb ground beef, turkey, or chicken
- ½ tsp salt
- ½ tsp black pepper
- 1 clove garlic, minced
- 1 tsp onion powder
- 1 tsp smoked paprika
- 1 tbsp Worcestershire sauce (optional)

For the Vegetarian Patties:

- 1 cup black beans, mashed
- ½ cup cooked quinoa or breadcrumbs
- 1 egg (or flax egg for vegan option)
- ½ tsp garlic powder
- ½ tsp smoked paprika
- ½ tsp cumin
- ½ tsp salt
- ¼ cup finely chopped parsley or cilantro

Alien-Inspired Toppings:

- Sliced avocado or guacamole (for the Slitheen's green hue)
- Sliced pickles or cucumber ribbons
- Green leaf lettuce or spinach
- Wasabi mayo or pesto sauce
- Sliced roasted red peppers (for a burst of color)
- Fried onion strings or crispy shallots (to mimic alien textures)
- Edible glitter or shimmer powder (optional, for a galactic touch)

For the Slider Buns:

- 12 mini slider buns (regular or gluten-free)
- 1 tbsp butter or olive oil (for toasting)

Instructions: Crafting Slitheen Sliders
Step 1: Prepare the Patties
For Meat Patties:

1. In a large mixing bowl, combine the ground meat, salt, pepper, garlic, onion powder, smoked paprika, and Worcestershire sauce. Mix gently to avoid overworking the meat.
2. Divide the mixture into 12 equal portions and shape each into a small patty, about 2 inches in diameter.
3. Chill the patties in the refrigerator for 15 minutes to help them hold their shape.

For Vegetarian Patties:

1. In a medium bowl, combine the mashed black beans, quinoa or breadcrumbs, egg, garlic powder, smoked paprika, cumin, salt, and parsley. Mix until well combined.
2. Shape the mixture into 12 small patties. If the mixture is too sticky, add more breadcrumbs.
3. Chill the patties in the refrigerator for 15 minutes to firm up.

Step 2: Cook the Patties

1. Heat a large skillet or grill pan over medium-high heat. Lightly oil the surface.
2. Cook the meat patties for 2-3 minutes per side, or until fully cooked (internal temperature of 160°F/71°C for beef or 165°F/74°C for poultry).
3. For vegetarian patties, cook for 3-4 minutes per side until golden brown and slightly crispy.

Step 3: Toast the Buns

1. Slice the slider buns in half and lightly toast the cut sides in a skillet with butter or olive oil.
2. Toasting the buns adds texture and prevents them from becoming soggy when layered with toppings.

Step 4: Assemble the Sliders

1. Spread a layer of your chosen sauce (wasabi mayo, pesto, or guacamole) on the bottom bun.
2. Add a patty, then layer with toppings such as avocado slices, pickles, roasted red peppers, and crispy onion strings.
3. Finish with a leaf of lettuce or spinach for a pop of color, and top with the other half of the bun.

Variations and Customizations
1. Galactic Vegan Sliders:

- Use the vegetarian patty recipe and substitute the egg with a flax egg (1 tbsp ground flaxseed mixed with 3 tbsp water).
- Opt for vegan mayo or hummus as a sauce and serve on gluten-free buns or lettuce wraps.

2. Spicy Slitheen Sliders:

- Add sliced jalapeños or a drizzle of sriracha to the toppings for a fiery kick.
- Use a chipotle aioli as the sauce for smoky heat.

3. Gourmet Sliders:

- Top with brie or goat cheese for a rich, creamy flavor.
- Use caramelized onions and truffle aioli for an elevated taste.

Presentation Ideas

- **Alien Vibes:** Arrange the sliders on a platter lined with green cabbage leaves to mimic the Slitheen's color.
- **Themed Picks:** Use decorative toothpicks or skewers shaped like alien ships, stars, or planets to hold the sliders together.
- **Galactic Glitter:** Dust the buns lightly with edible shimmer powder to give them a cosmic, otherworldly look.

Serving Suggestions
Pair the sliders with sides that complement their playful theme, such as:

- **"Asteroid Fries"**: Crispy sweet potato or regular fries dusted with smoked paprika.
- **"Time Vortex Slaw"**: A colorful coleslaw with purple cabbage, carrots, and a tangy lime dressing.
- **"Raxacoricofallapatorian Dips"**: Serve with a trio of dipping sauces like guacamole, spicy aioli, and a creamy herb dip.

The Whovian Experience
Slitheen Sliders are more than just burgers—they're a tribute to the humor, creativity, and charm of *Doctor Who*. With their vibrant colors, alien-inspired toppings, and bite-sized appeal, these sliders are sure to delight fans of all ages.

So, gather your companions, fire up the grill, and let these sliders transport your taste buds to a galaxy far, far away. Just remember: no fart jokes at the table, no matter how tempting!

Allons-y!

Chapter 12: Yule Logs of Gallifrey

The Yule log is a beloved holiday dessert, rich in tradition and flavor, but here we give it a Gallifreyan twist worthy of the Time Lords themselves. The Yule Logs of Gallifrey combine the classic rolled sponge and creamy filling with a swirling time vortex design and celestial decorations. This chapter walks you through the steps to create a stunning centerpiece dessert inspired by Gallifrey's golden skies and swirling time vortexes.

The Concept: A Timeless Dessert

The traditional Yule log, or *bûche de Noël*, becomes a visual and flavorful tribute to the home of the Time Lords. By incorporating a swirling time vortex design into the cake and adorning it with Gallifreyan-inspired decorations, this dessert transforms into a show-stopping masterpiece that's as delicious as it is dazzling.

Ingredients for the Yule Logs of Gallifrey

For the Sponge Cake (Vanilla or Chocolate):

- ¾ cup all-purpose flour
- ¼ cup cocoa powder (for chocolate sponge, optional)
- 1 tsp baking powder
- ¼ tsp salt
- 4 large eggs, separated
- ¾ cup granulated sugar
- 1 tsp vanilla extract
- 2 tbsp milk
- Gel food coloring (gold, orange, and black for time vortex effect)

For the Filling (Whipped Cream or Buttercream):

- 1 cup heavy whipping cream (or 1 cup butter for buttercream)
- 3 tbsp powdered sugar
- 1 tsp vanilla extract
- Optional flavor additions: orange zest, espresso powder, or cinnamon

For the Frosting:

- 1 cup heavy whipping cream or 1 cup butter (softened)
- 2 cups powdered sugar
- ½ cup cocoa powder (for chocolate frosting)
- 1 tsp vanilla extract

For Decorations:

- Edible gold glitter or luster dust
- Edible star-shaped sprinkles
- Gold and silver dragees
- Gallifreyan symbols piped in melted chocolate or white chocolate

Instructions: Crafting Yule Logs of Gallifrey
Step 1: Prepare the Swirling Time Vortex Sponge Cake

1. **Preheat and Prepare**:
   ◦ Preheat your oven to 350°F (175°C). Grease a 10x15-inch jelly roll pan and line it with parchment paper.
2. **Make the Batter**:
   ◦ In a medium bowl, sift together the flour, baking powder, salt, and cocoa powder (if using).
   ◦ In a large bowl, beat the egg yolks and half the sugar until pale and thick. Stir in the vanilla and milk.
   ◦ In another bowl, beat the egg whites until soft peaks form. Gradually add the remaining sugar, beating until stiff peaks form.
   ◦ Gently fold the egg whites into the yolk mixture, then fold in the dry ingredients until just combined.
3. **Create the Time Vortex Design**:
   ◦ Divide the batter into three portions. Leave one plain (or chocolate, depending on your base flavor). Tint the second portion gold and the third black with gel food coloring.
   ◦ Spread the plain batter evenly over the prepared pan. Using a spoon or piping bag, drizzle the gold and black batters over the top in swirling, vortex-like patterns. Use a skewer to gently swirl the colors together, mimicking a time vortex.
4. **Bake and Roll**:
   ◦ Bake for 10-12 minutes, or until the sponge springs back when lightly touched.
   ◦ While the cake is still warm, invert it onto a clean kitchen towel dusted with powdered sugar. Peel off the parchment paper and roll the cake (with the towel) into a log shape. Let it cool completely.

Step 2: Prepare the Filling and Frosting

1. **For Whipped Cream Filling**:
   ◦ Beat the heavy cream, powdered sugar, and vanilla extract until stiff peaks form. Fold in any optional flavor additions.
2. **For Buttercream Filling**:
   ◦ Beat the softened butter until fluffy, then gradually add powdered sugar and vanilla extract. Add orange zest, espresso powder, or cinnamon for extra flavor.
3. **For the Frosting**:
   ◦ Whip the heavy cream (for whipped cream frosting) or beat the butter and powdered sugar with cocoa powder and vanilla (for buttercream frosting) until smooth. Adjust consistency with a splash of milk if needed.

Step 3: Assemble the Yule Log

1. **Unroll and Fill**:
   ◦ Carefully unroll the cooled sponge cake. Spread an even layer of the filling across the surface, leaving a small border around the edges.
2. **Re-roll the Cake**:
   ◦ Roll the cake back up tightly, using the towel to guide it. Trim the ends for a clean finish.
3. **Frost the Log**:
   ◦ Spread the frosting over the log, using a spatula to create bark-like textures. If desired, reserve some frosting for piping Gallifreyan symbols or additional decorations.

Step 4: Decorate with Gallifreyan Elegance

1. **Add Gallifreyan Symbols**:
   ◦ Melt white or dark chocolate and pipe Gallifreyan-inspired symbols onto parchment paper. Once set, attach them to the log.
2. **Add the Cosmic Touch**:
   ◦ Dust the log with edible gold glitter or luster dust to mimic Gallifrey's golden skies.
   ◦ Sprinkle edible stars and dragees over the log for a celestial effect.
3. **Final Touches**:
   ◦ Add chocolate shards, sugared cranberries, or small sprigs of rosemary to enhance the natural aesthetic.

Tips for Perfect Yule Logs

- **Swirl Mastery**: Use light, swirling motions when creating the time vortex design to avoid overmixing the colors.
- **Gentle Rolling**: Roll the cake while warm to prevent cracks, and let it cool completely in its rolled shape.
- **Flavor Variations**: Try adding matcha powder for a green Gallifreyan twist or espresso for a bold flavor.
- **Decorating Creativity**: Use edible metallic paints to enhance Gallifreyan symbols or create intricate patterns on the log.

Serving and Presentation Ideas

- **Themed Display**: Serve the Yule Log on a gold platter surrounded by star-shaped sugar cookies or shimmering candy.
- **Time Lord Touch**: Add a TARDIS figurine or small edible clock pieces to the display for extra *Doctor Who* flair.
- **Interactive Dessert**: Encourage guests to guess the flavors and discuss the design as part of the experience.

The Whovian Experience

The Yule Logs of Gallifrey combine tradition with innovation, much like the Time Lords themselves. With its swirling time vortex design, rich flavors, and celestial decorations, this dessert is a feast for both the eyes and the taste buds.

As you slice into the log and reveal the swirling patterns, you'll feel as though you're cutting into a piece of Gallifreyan history. Share this dessert with friends and family, and let the magic of Gallifrey inspire your holiday celebrations.

Allons-y!

Chapter 13: Zygon Spiced Bread

The Zygons, with their shape-shifting abilities and deep connection to their heritage, inspire this dense, flavorful bread. Drawing from the richness of their alien culture, Zygon Spiced Bread features bold spices and hearty textures, creating a loaf that feels like it has been passed down through generations. This bread is the perfect accompaniment to warm holiday soups, stews, or even as a stand-alone snack, making it a versatile addition to your *Doctor Who*-inspired culinary adventures.

The Concept: Bread with a Zygon Twist

Zygon Spiced Bread takes its cues from the earthy, robust nature of Zygon culture, blending spices and rich flavors to create a dense, satisfying loaf. Its hearty texture makes it ideal for pairing with comforting holiday dishes, while its unique spice blend offers a distinct twist that sets it apart from traditional breads.

Ingredients for Zygon Spiced Bread
For the Bread Dough (Yields 1 Loaf):

- 3 cups all-purpose flour (or a mix of whole wheat and all-purpose for a heartier texture)
- 1 ½ tsp salt
- 1 tsp ground cinnamon
- ½ tsp ground nutmeg
- ½ tsp ground cloves
- 1 tsp ground ginger
- 1 tbsp granulated sugar
- 2 tsp instant yeast
- 1 cup warm water (about 110°F/43°C)
- 2 tbsp olive oil
- ¼ cup molasses or dark honey

Optional Add-Ins for Texture and Flavor:

- ½ cup chopped nuts (e.g., walnuts, pecans)
- ½ cup dried fruits (e.g., raisins, cranberries)
- 2 tbsp sunflower or pumpkin seeds

Instructions: Crafting Zygon Spiced Bread
Step 1: Activate the Yeast

1. In a small bowl, mix the warm water and sugar, then sprinkle the yeast over the top. Let it sit for 5-10 minutes until it becomes frothy. This step ensures the yeast is active and ready to work.

Step 2: Mix the Dough

1. In a large mixing bowl, combine the flour, salt, cinnamon, nutmeg, cloves, and ginger. Whisk to distribute the spices evenly.
2. Add the yeast mixture, olive oil, and molasses (or honey) to the dry ingredients. Stir with a wooden spoon or your hands until the dough comes together.

Step 3: Knead the Dough

1. Turn the dough out onto a floured surface and knead for 8-10 minutes, or until it becomes smooth and elastic. If using add-ins like nuts, dried fruits, or seeds, knead them into the dough during the final few minutes.
2. Place the kneaded dough in a lightly oiled bowl, turning it to coat the surface with oil. Cover with a damp cloth or plastic wrap and let it rise in a warm place for 1-1 ½ hours, or until doubled in size.

Step 4: Shape and Proof the Dough

1. Punch down the risen dough and turn it out onto a lightly floured surface. Shape it into a round boule or an elongated loaf, depending on your preference.
2. Place the shaped dough onto a parchment-lined baking sheet or into a greased loaf pan. Cover loosely with a cloth and let it proof for another 30-45 minutes, or until slightly puffed.

Step 5: Bake the Bread

1. Preheat your oven to 375°F (190°C). If desired, place a small pan of water on the bottom rack to create steam, which helps develop a crisp crust.
2. Bake the bread for 35-40 minutes, or until it sounds hollow when tapped on the bottom and has a deep golden-brown color.
3. Allow the bread to cool on a wire rack for at least 20 minutes before slicing.

Pairing Suggestions: Perfect for Soups and Stews

Zygon Spiced Bread's hearty texture and warm flavors make it an excellent companion to a variety of dishes. Here are some pairing ideas:

- **Holiday Soups:** Butternut squash soup, lentil soup, or a creamy tomato bisque.
- **Savory Stews:** Beef or vegetable stew, spiced chickpea curry, or mushroom ragout.
- **Cheese Boards:** Serve sliced spiced bread with a selection of cheeses, chutneys, and pickled vegetables for a unique appetizer.

Optional Variations

1. Sweet Zygon Bread:

- Increase the molasses to ⅓ cup and add ¼ cup brown sugar for a sweeter loaf.
- Incorporate more dried fruits, like dates or apricots, and finish with a glaze made of powdered sugar and orange juice.

2. Seeded Zygon Loaf:

- Add a mix of sunflower, flax, and sesame seeds to the dough for a nutty, textured bread. Sprinkle extra seeds on top before baking for added crunch.

3. Gluten-Free Option:

- Use a gluten-free flour blend designed for bread baking and follow the same process. Adjust liquid amounts as needed to achieve a dough-like consistency.

Tips for Perfect Zygon Spiced Bread

- **Warm Spices:** Adjust the spice levels to suit your taste. If you prefer milder flavors, reduce the amount of cloves and ginger.
- **Molasses Substitution:** If molasses is unavailable, dark honey or maple syrup can be used, though they will yield a slightly lighter flavor.
- **Proofing Environment:** Create a warm proofing environment by placing the bowl of dough in a turned-off oven with a bowl of hot water beneath it.

Presentation Ideas

- **Rustic Appeal:** Serve the bread in a basket lined with a green or gold cloth to reflect Zygon colors.
- **Themed Table:** Pair with a centerpiece inspired by the Zygon's earthy tones and textures, such as moss, wood, or stone elements.
- **Decorative Topping:** Before baking, score the top of the bread with swirling patterns reminiscent of Zygon tentacles.

The Whovian Experience

Zygon Spiced Bread is more than a loaf; it's a tribute to the rich and mysterious culture of one of the *Doctor Who* universe's most fascinating alien species. Its bold flavors and dense texture offer comfort and depth, perfect for the holiday season or any time you want to elevate your meal with a unique twist.

As you slice into the warm, aromatic bread, you'll feel a connection to the Zygons' earthy roots and complex traditions. Serve it with pride, and watch as your guests are transported to a galaxy of flavor.

Allons-y!

Chapter 14: The Master's Mischievous Macarons

The Master, with their cunning schemes and flair for the dramatic, serves as the perfect inspiration for these mischievously decadent macarons. These delicate, colorful treats are filled with a rich, sinister chocolate ganache that embodies the Master's dark allure. While macarons are notorious for their tricky technique, this chapter will guide you through the process step by step, ensuring success as you create these whimsical yet decadent confections.

The Concept: Macarons as Mischief

Macarons are the perfect dessert for capturing the Master's personality—deceptively delicate on the outside, but hiding a bold, decadent center. These macarons, with their vibrant shells and dark chocolate ganache filling, are as elegant and dramatic as the Master's many schemes.

Ingredients for The Master's Mischievous Macarons
For the Macaron Shells:

- 1 ¾ cups (175 g) powdered sugar
- 1 cup (100 g) almond flour
- 3 large egg whites, room temperature
- ¼ cup (50 g) granulated sugar
- ½ tsp vanilla extract or almond extract
- Gel food coloring (red, black, or dark purple for a sinister look)

For the Sinister Chocolate Ganache:

- ½ cup (120 ml) heavy cream
- 4 oz (115 g) dark chocolate (60-70% cacao), finely chopped
- 1 tbsp unsalted butter, softened
- 1 tsp instant espresso powder (optional, for added depth)

Instructions: Crafting The Master's Mischievous Macarons
Step 1: Prepare the Macaron Shells

1. **Sift the Dry Ingredients:**
   - Sift the powdered sugar and almond flour together into a large bowl. Discard any large almond pieces that remain in the sieve. This step ensures a smooth shell.
2. **Whip the Egg Whites:**
   - In a clean, grease-free mixing bowl, beat the egg whites on medium speed until foamy. Gradually add the granulated sugar, 1 tablespoon at a time, and increase the speed to high.
   - Continue beating until stiff, glossy peaks form. Add the vanilla or almond extract and a few drops of gel food coloring, beating just until incorporated.
3. **Macaronage (Mixing the Batter):**
   - Add the sifted almond flour and powdered sugar mixture to the whipped egg whites in two additions.
   - Gently fold the mixture using a rubber spatula, scraping around the bowl and cutting through the center. Continue folding until the batter flows like lava—when dropped from the spatula, it should form a ribbon that slowly reincorporates into the batter.
4. **Pipe the Shells:**
   - Transfer the batter to a piping bag fitted with a round tip. Pipe 1-inch circles onto a parchment-lined baking sheet, spacing them about 1 inch apart.
   - Tap the baking sheet firmly on the counter a few times to release any air bubbles. Use a toothpick to pop any visible bubbles on the surface.
5. **Rest the Shells:**
   - Let the piped macarons rest at room temperature for 30-60 minutes, or until the tops form a dry, slightly matte skin. This step is crucial for achieving the signature "feet."
6. **Bake the Shells:**
   - Preheat the oven to 300°F (150°C). Bake the macarons for 14-16 minutes, rotating the tray halfway through.
   - The macarons are done when the tops are firm and the "feet" are set. Allow them to cool completely on the baking sheet before removing.

Step 2: Make the Sinister Chocolate Ganache

1. **Heat the Cream:**
   - In a small saucepan, heat the heavy cream until it just begins to simmer.
2. **Melt the Chocolate:**
   - Place the chopped dark chocolate and instant espresso powder (if using) in a heatproof bowl. Pour the hot cream over the chocolate and let it sit for 2-3 minutes.
   - Stir gently until the chocolate is fully melted and smooth. Stir in the butter until incorporated.

3. **Cool the Ganache:**
    ◦ Let the ganache cool at room temperature until it thickens to a spreadable consistency. For faster cooling, refrigerate for 10-15 minutes, stirring occasionally.

Step 3: Assemble the Macarons

1. **Pair the Shells:**
    ◦ Match the macaron shells in pairs of similar size.
2. **Fill the Macarons:**
    ◦ Transfer the ganache to a piping bag fitted with a small round tip. Pipe a small dollop of ganache onto the flat side of one shell, then gently press the matching shell on top, twisting slightly to spread the filling evenly.
3. **Mature the Macarons:**
    ◦ Place the assembled macarons in an airtight container and refrigerate for 24-48 hours. This resting period allows the flavors to meld and the texture to soften for the perfect bite.

Tips for Mastering Macarons

- **Use Room-Temperature Ingredients:** Ensure the egg whites are at room temperature for better volume.
- **Weigh Ingredients Precisely:** Macarons are delicate and require precision. Use a kitchen scale for accurate measurements.
- **Perfect Your Macaronage:** Overmixing or undermixing the batter can ruin the shells. Look for the lava-like consistency as your guide.
- **Resting Time Matters:** Don't skip the resting step—it's essential for creating the "feet" on the shells.
- **Experiment with Colors:** Use gel food coloring sparingly, as liquid food coloring can affect the consistency of the batter.

Decorating Ideas

- **Sinister Swirls:** Add a streak of black or red food coloring to the piping bag to create a marbled effect on the shells.
- **Edible Glitter:** Dust the shells with edible gold or silver glitter for a dramatic, galactic look.
- **Chocolate Webbing:** Drizzle melted chocolate in a web pattern over the shells for a villainous touch.
- **Gallifreyan Symbols:** Pipe Gallifreyan-inspired designs onto the shells with edible metallic paint or melted white chocolate.

Serving and Presentation

- **Villainous Display:** Arrange the macarons on a dark platter surrounded by small LED lights to evoke a sinister atmosphere.
- **Themed Party:** Pair the macarons with other *Doctor Who*-inspired treats, like TARDIS Blueberry Muffins or Dalek Chocolate Truffles.
- **Gift Idea:** Package the macarons in a black or red box with a ribbon for an elegant and mysterious edible gift.

The Whovian Experience

The Master's Mischievous Macarons are more than just a dessert—they're a testament to the precision, drama, and flair of one of *Doctor Who*'s most iconic characters. With their delicate shells, bold colors, and decadent ganache filling, these macarons are sure to impress fans and foodies alike.

As you bite into the crisp shell and rich, creamy center, you'll feel the mischievous spirit of the Master come alive. These macarons aren't just a treat; they're an adventure in baking, artistry, and the delicious side of villainy.

Allons-y!

Chapter 15: Snowcap Cupcakes from Trenzalore

Trenzalore, the somber yet beautiful snowy world from *Doctor Who*, serves as the inspiration for these elegant Snowcap Cupcakes. These white chocolate cupcakes are as light and ethereal as freshly fallen snow, while their decoration evokes the snowy peaks and frosty landscape of this iconic planet. Perfect for winter gatherings, holiday parties, or simply indulging your love of all things *Doctor Who*, these cupcakes blend flavor, creativity, and a touch of whimsy.

The Concept: Snowy Elegance Meets Indulgence

The Snowcap Cupcakes are designed to capture the serene beauty of Trenzalore's endless winter. Fluffy white chocolate sponge serves as the base, topped with a creamy white frosting that mimics snow-covered peaks. Add a sprinkle of shimmer and a few clever decorations, and these cupcakes become an edible tribute to one of the most hauntingly memorable settings in the Doctor's adventures.

Ingredients for Snowcap Cupcakes
For the White Chocolate Cupcakes (Yields 12):

- 1 ½ cups all-purpose flour
- 1 ½ tsp baking powder
- ¼ tsp salt
- ½ cup unsalted butter, softened
- ¾ cup granulated sugar
- 2 large eggs, room temperature
- 1 tsp vanilla extract
- ½ cup whole milk, room temperature
- 3 oz white chocolate, melted and slightly cooled

For the Snowy White Frosting:

- 1 cup unsalted butter, softened
- 3 cups powdered sugar, sifted
- 1 tsp vanilla extract
- 2-3 tbsp heavy cream or milk
- 3 oz white chocolate, melted and slightly cooled

For the Decorations:

- Edible glitter or shimmer dust (white or silver)
- Shredded coconut or white sprinkles (for a snow effect)
- Mini marshmallows (to mimic snowballs)
- Sugar or fondant stars (optional, for a celestial touch)
- Blue-tinted sugar crystals (to evoke an icy landscape)

Instructions: Crafting Snowcap Cupcakes
Step 1: Prepare the White Chocolate Cupcakes

1. **Preheat and Prepare:**
    ◦ Preheat your oven to 350°F (175°C) and line a 12-cup muffin tin with cupcake liners.
2. **Mix the Dry Ingredients:**
    ◦ In a medium bowl, whisk together the flour, baking powder, and salt. Set aside.
3. **Cream Butter and Sugar:**
    ◦ In a large mixing bowl, beat the butter and sugar together with an electric mixer until light and fluffy, about 2-3 minutes.
4. **Add Eggs and Vanilla:**
    ◦ Beat in the eggs one at a time, then mix in the vanilla extract until smooth.
5. **Incorporate the White Chocolate:**
    ◦ Slowly mix in the melted white chocolate, ensuring it's fully combined with the batter.
6. **Alternate Wet and Dry Ingredients:**
    ◦ Add the dry ingredients to the wet mixture in three additions, alternating with the milk. Begin and end with the dry ingredients, mixing just until combined.
7. **Bake the Cupcakes:**
    ◦ Divide the batter evenly among the cupcake liners, filling each about two-thirds full.
    ◦ Bake for 18-20 minutes, or until a toothpick inserted into the center comes out clean.
    ◦ Allow the cupcakes to cool in the pan for 5 minutes, then transfer them to a wire rack to cool completely.

Step 2: Make the Snowy White Frosting

1. **Cream the Butter:**
    ◦ In a large bowl, beat the softened butter with an electric mixer until smooth and creamy.
2. **Add Powdered Sugar and Vanilla:**
    ◦ Gradually add the powdered sugar, 1 cup at a time, mixing on low speed until fully incorporated. Mix in the vanilla extract.
3. **Incorporate the White Chocolate:**
    ◦ Slowly pour in the melted white chocolate and mix until combined.
4. **Adjust Consistency:**
    ◦ Add the heavy cream or milk, 1 tablespoon at a time, until the frosting reaches a spreadable consistency.

Step 3: Decorate the Cupcakes

1. **Frost the Cupcakes:**
   ◦ Use a piping bag fitted with a star tip to swirl the frosting onto the cooled cupcakes, creating peaks that mimic snow-covered mountains.
2. **Add Snow Effects:**
   ◦ Sprinkle shredded coconut or white sprinkles over the frosting to create a snowy texture.
3. **Add Glitter and Shimmer:**
   ◦ Dust the cupcakes with edible glitter or shimmer dust for a frosty, celestial look.
4. **Create Snowballs and Peaks:**
   ◦ Top each cupcake with a mini marshmallow or two to resemble snowballs. Use sugar or fondant stars for an extra touch of magic.
5. **Finish with Icy Accents:**
   ◦ Sprinkle blue-tinted sugar crystals around the base of the frosting to evoke the icy landscape of Trenzalore.

Tips for Perfect Snowcap Cupcakes

- **Room Temperature Ingredients:** Ensure the eggs, butter, and milk are at room temperature for a smoother batter.
- **Melt White Chocolate Carefully:** Melt the white chocolate slowly in a microwave or double boiler to prevent it from seizing. Allow it to cool slightly before adding it to the batter or frosting.
- **Frosting Consistency:** If the frosting is too soft, refrigerate it for 10-15 minutes before piping.
- **Snowy Texture:** For a fluffier snow effect, lightly toast shredded coconut before sprinkling it over the frosting.

Serving and Presentation Ideas

- **Snowy Display:** Arrange the cupcakes on a platter dusted with powdered sugar to mimic fresh snow.
- **Themed Table:** Surround the cupcakes with mini pine trees, LED fairy lights, or a small TARDIS figurine for a Trenzalore-inspired setting.
- **Edible Snow Globe:** Serve the cupcakes in clear cloche domes for a whimsical, snow globe effect.

The Whovian Experience

Snowcap Cupcakes from Trenzalore bring the magic and mystery of this snowy world to life in every bite. Their delicate white chocolate flavor, combined with the frosty decoration, makes them an unforgettable addition to any winter celebration or *Doctor Who*-themed event.

As you enjoy these cupcakes, let your imagination wander to the snowy peaks and quiet beauty of Trenzalore. They're not just a dessert; they're an edible tribute to one of the Doctor's most poignant adventures.

Allons-y!

Chapter 16: Silence Soufflé

The Silence, mysterious and unforgettable (at least until you look away), inspire this light and airy soufflé—a dish that's memorable for all the right reasons. Whether you prefer a rich, savory soufflé or a sweet and delicate one, this recipe offers options to suit every palate. While soufflés may seem intimidating, this chapter provides detailed instructions and tips to ensure success, resulting in a dish that rises beautifully and leaves a lasting impression, even if its namesake doesn't.

The Concept: Airy Elegance That Defies Gravity

The Silence Soufflé is all about balance—light, fluffy textures combined with bold flavors. Like the enigmatic Silence, these soufflés command attention with their dramatic rise and delicate structure. Whether you choose a savory cheese-filled version or a sweet chocolate delight, this dish promises to be the centerpiece of your meal or dessert table.

Ingredients for Silence Soufflé
For the Base (Serves 4-6):
Savory Soufflé Base:

- 2 tbsp unsalted butter, plus more for greasing the ramekins
- 2 tbsp all-purpose flour
- 1 cup whole milk, warmed
- ½ tsp salt
- ¼ tsp ground nutmeg (optional)
- 3 large egg yolks
- ½ cup grated Gruyère, cheddar, or Parmesan cheese (for a cheesy soufflé)

Sweet Soufflé Base:

- 2 tbsp unsalted butter, plus more for greasing the ramekins
- 2 tbsp all-purpose flour
- 1 cup whole milk, warmed
- 3 tbsp granulated sugar (or more, for sweeter soufflés)
- 3 large egg yolks
- ½ tsp vanilla extract or orange zest (optional)

For the Egg Whites:

- 4 large egg whites
- ¼ tsp cream of tartar or ½ tsp lemon juice (for stability)
- Pinch of salt

Instructions: Crafting Silence Soufflé
Step 1: Prepare the Ramekins

1. Preheat your oven to 375°F (190°C). Place a baking sheet on the center rack to preheat.
2. Grease 4-6 ramekins (6-ounce capacity) generously with butter, ensuring you coat the sides evenly to help the soufflé rise. Dust the insides with grated cheese (for savory) or granulated sugar (for sweet), tapping out the excess.

Step 2: Make the Base Mixture
For Savory Soufflé:

1. Melt the butter in a medium saucepan over medium heat. Add the flour and whisk constantly for 1-2 minutes to create a roux.
2. Gradually add the warmed milk, whisking to combine. Cook until the mixture thickens to a smooth, creamy consistency.
3. Remove from heat and stir in the salt, nutmeg (if using), and cheese until melted. Let the mixture cool slightly, then whisk in the egg yolks one at a time.

For Sweet Soufflé:

1. Melt the butter in a medium saucepan over medium heat. Add the flour and whisk for 1-2 minutes to create a roux.
2. Gradually add the warmed milk, whisking until smooth and thickened.
3. Remove from heat and stir in the sugar and vanilla extract or orange zest. Let the mixture cool slightly, then whisk in the egg yolks one at a time.

Step 3: Whip the Egg Whites

1. In a clean, grease-free bowl, beat the egg whites with a pinch of salt and cream of tartar (or lemon juice) until soft peaks form. Gradually add 1-2 tablespoons of sugar (for sweet soufflé) or leave unsweetened (for savory soufflé). Continue beating until stiff, glossy peaks form.

Step 4: Fold and Fill

1. Gently fold one-third of the whipped egg whites into the base mixture to lighten it.
2. Add the remaining egg whites in two additions, folding gently but thoroughly to preserve the airiness.
3. Divide the mixture evenly among the prepared ramekins, filling them about three-quarters full. Use a spatula to smooth the tops, then run your thumb around the inside rim to create a small trench (this helps the soufflé rise evenly).

Step 5: Bake and Serve

1. Place the ramekins on the preheated baking sheet in the oven. Bake for 18-22 minutes, or until the soufflés have risen and the tops are golden brown. Avoid opening the oven door while baking to prevent them from deflating.
2. Serve immediately, as soufflés begin to deflate within minutes of being removed from the oven.

Savory and Sweet Variations
Savory Silence Soufflé Variations:

- **Spinach and Feta:** Add ½ cup chopped, cooked spinach and ¼ cup crumbled feta to the base mixture.
- **Smoked Salmon and Dill:** Fold ½ cup flaked smoked salmon and 1 tsp fresh dill into the base.
- **Mushroom and Gruyère:** Sauté ½ cup finely chopped mushrooms and mix them into the base with Gruyère.

Sweet Silence Soufflé Variations:

- **Chocolate:** Replace 2 tbsp flour with cocoa powder and add 2 oz melted dark chocolate to the base mixture.
- **Lemon:** Add 1 tsp lemon zest and replace half the milk with fresh lemon juice. Serve with powdered sugar and berries.
- **Raspberry:** Fold ½ cup mashed raspberries into the base and dust with powdered sugar before serving.

Tips for Mastering the Soufflé Process

- **Room Temperature Ingredients:** Ensure eggs are at room temperature for better volume and even mixing.
- **Stable Peaks:** Use cream of tartar or lemon juice to stabilize egg whites and ensure a strong rise.
- **Gentle Folding:** Fold carefully to preserve air in the mixture; overmixing will deflate the batter.
- **Serve Immediately:** Soufflés are best enjoyed fresh out of the oven, as they will deflate over time.

Serving and Presentation Ideas

- **For Savory Soufflés:** Serve with a light salad, crusty bread, or roasted vegetables for a complete meal.
- **For Sweet Soufflés:** Dust with powdered sugar and serve with whipped cream, chocolate sauce, or a fruit compote.
- **Themed Display:** Place the ramekins on a dark tray surrounded by small lights or edible decorations inspired by *Doctor Who*.

The Whovian Experience

Silence Soufflé brings elegance and drama to your table, just like its enigmatic namesake. With their towering rise and delicate texture, these soufflés are sure to impress guests and become a highlight of any meal.

As you savor each bite, let yourself be transported to a mysterious world of flavor and finesse—a dessert or savory delight that's truly unforgettable (even if its namesake isn't).

Allons-y!

Chapter 17: Vashta Nerada Black Forest Cake

Inspired by the eerie and shadowy Vashta Nerada from *Doctor Who*, this decadent Black Forest cake is a luxurious dessert with a dark twist. Rich layers of chocolate sponge, luscious cherry filling, and whipped cream come together to create a show-stopping cake. Dark chocolate "shadows" add an ominous elegance, while edible stars provide a celestial touch, making this cake both hauntingly beautiful and irresistibly delicious.

The Concept: A Dark and Decadent Delight

The Vashta Nerada, lurking in the shadows and representing the unseen terrors of the universe, are brought to life in this dessert through deep, dark chocolate tones and dramatic decorations. This Black Forest cake captures their mystery while infusing it with indulgent flavors, creating a dessert that's perfect for *Doctor Who* fans and chocolate lovers alike.

Ingredients for Vashta Nerada Black Forest Cake
For the Chocolate Sponge (Three 8-inch Layers):

- 1 ¾ cups all-purpose flour
- ¾ cup unsweetened cocoa powder (Dutch-processed for richer flavor)
- 1 ½ tsp baking powder
- 1 ½ tsp baking soda
- ½ tsp salt
- 2 cups granulated sugar
- 2 large eggs
- 1 cup whole milk, room temperature
- ½ cup vegetable oil
- 2 tsp vanilla extract
- 1 cup boiling water

For the Cherry Filling:

- 2 cups pitted cherries (fresh or frozen)
- ½ cup granulated sugar
- 1 tbsp cornstarch mixed with 2 tbsp water
- 1 tbsp kirsch (optional, for authentic flavor)

For the Whipped Cream Frosting:

- 2 cups heavy whipping cream, chilled
- ¼ cup powdered sugar
- 1 tsp vanilla extract

For the Dark Chocolate "Shadows":

- 6 oz dark chocolate, melted
- Edible silver or gold luster dust (optional)

For the Garnish:

- Edible stars or silver dragees
- Shaved dark chocolate
- Whole cherries

Instructions: Crafting Vashta Nerada Black Forest Cake
Step 1: Prepare the Chocolate Sponge

1. **Preheat and Prepare Pans:**
   - Preheat your oven to 350°F (175°C). Grease and line three 8-inch round cake pans with parchment paper.
2. **Mix Dry Ingredients:**
   - In a large bowl, sift together the flour, cocoa powder, baking powder, baking soda, and salt. Whisk to combine.
3. **Combine Wet Ingredients:**
   - In another large bowl, beat the sugar and eggs until pale and fluffy. Add the milk, oil, and vanilla extract, mixing until smooth.
4. **Combine Dry and Wet Ingredients:**
   - Gradually add the dry ingredients to the wet mixture, mixing until just combined. Stir in the boiling water slowly to create a thin batter.
5. **Bake the Cakes:**
   - Divide the batter evenly among the prepared pans. Bake for 25-30 minutes, or until a toothpick inserted in the center comes out clean.
   - Let the cakes cool in the pans for 10 minutes before transferring them to a wire rack to cool completely.

Step 2: Prepare the Cherry Filling

1. **Cook the Cherries:**
   - In a medium saucepan, combine the cherries and sugar. Cook over medium heat until the cherries release their juices and begin to soften.
2. **Thicken the Filling:**
   - Stir in the cornstarch-water mixture and cook until the mixture thickens. If using kirsch, stir it in after removing the filling from heat.
   - Let the filling cool completely before using.

Step 3: Make the Whipped Cream Frosting

1. **Whip the Cream:**
   - In a chilled mixing bowl, beat the heavy cream, powdered sugar, and vanilla extract until stiff peaks form. Be careful not to overwhip.

Step 4: Assemble the Cake

1. **Level the Layers:**
   - If necessary, level the tops of the cake layers with a serrated knife to create even surfaces.
2. **Layer the Cake:**
   - Place the first cake layer on a serving plate. Spread a thin layer of whipped cream, followed by half of the cherry filling. Repeat with the second layer. Top with the third layer and spread a thin layer of whipped cream to create a crumb coat. Chill the cake for 30 minutes.
3. **Frost the Cake:**
   - Spread the remaining whipped cream evenly over the top and sides of the cake. Smooth the frosting with an offset spatula for a clean finish.

Step 5: Create the Dark Chocolate "Shadows"

1. **Make Chocolate Decorations:**
   - Spread melted dark chocolate onto a parchment-lined baking sheet in thin, jagged shapes resembling shadows or tendrils. Allow to set at room temperature or in the refrigerator until firm.
2. **Add Luster Dust:**
   - Optional: Dust the hardened chocolate with edible silver or gold luster dust for a celestial effect.
3. **Decorate the Cake:**
   - Arrange the chocolate "shadows" around the edges of the cake and on top for dramatic flair.

Step 6: Add Garnishes

1. **Finish with Edible Stars:**
   - Sprinkle edible stars or silver dragees over the top of the cake to mimic a starry sky.
2. **Add Shaved Chocolate and Cherries:**
   - Sprinkle the top with shaved dark chocolate and garnish with whole cherries for a classic Black Forest look.

Tips for Perfect Vashta Nerada Black Forest Cake

- **Room Temperature Ingredients:** Ensure eggs, milk, and other ingredients are at room temperature for a smoother batter.
- **Moist Cakes:** Brush the cake layers with a simple syrup or kirsch to keep them moist and flavorful.
- **Sharp Edges:** Use a bench scraper or offset spatula to achieve clean edges on the frosting.

- **Chocolate Shadows:** For extra dimension, shape the melted chocolate into curved tendrils using a rolling pin or the back of a spoon before it sets.

Serving and Presentation Ideas

- **Themed Display:** Serve the cake on a black or silver cake stand with small LED lights to create a shadowy, otherworldly atmosphere.
- **Interactive Dessert:** Slice the cake at the table to reveal its layers, emphasizing the rich contrast of chocolate, whipped cream, and cherries.
- **Individual Touches:** Create mini Vashta Nerada cakes by using the same recipe to make cupcakes with chocolate "shadow" toppers.

The Whovian Experience

The Vashta Nerada Black Forest Cake is more than a dessert; it's an edible journey into the mysterious, shadowy corners of the *Doctor Who* universe. With its rich chocolate layers, vibrant cherry filling, and dramatic decorations, this cake will captivate guests and transport them to a world where flavor and intrigue collide.

So, cut yourself a slice, savor the darkness, and remember: **"Stay out of the shadows!"**
Allons-y!

Chapter 18: K-9 Canine Crunchers

Inspired by the loyal and beloved robotic companion K-9 from *Doctor Who*, these pet-friendly cookies are the perfect treat for your furry friends. Made with wholesome, dog-safe ingredients, K-9 Canine Crunchers are as nutritious as they are fun to make. This chapter not only provides a detailed recipe for these delightful dog biscuits but also includes a guide to decorating them to look like adorable replicas of the Doctor's trusty K-9.

The Concept: A Treat for Your Best Friend

K-9 symbolizes loyalty, intelligence, and a touch of charm—qualities every pet owner recognizes in their furry companions. These cookies are designed to celebrate that bond while ensuring your pet enjoys a healthy, safe, and tasty snack. With a little creativity, you can even decorate the cookies to resemble K-9, bringing a bit of *Doctor Who* magic to your pet's treat time.

Ingredients for K-9 Canine Crunchers
Basic Dog Biscuit Dough (Yields ~20 biscuits):

- 2 cups whole wheat flour (or oat flour for gluten-sensitive dogs)
- ½ cup rolled oats
- ½ cup unsweetened applesauce or mashed banana
- ¼ cup peanut butter (natural, unsweetened, and xylitol-free)
- 1 large egg
- ⅓ cup water or low-sodium chicken broth (adjust as needed)
- Optional: 1 tsp ground cinnamon (for flavor)

Instructions: Crafting K-9 Canine Crunchers
Step 1: Prepare the Dough

1. **Mix the Dry Ingredients:**
   - In a large mixing bowl, combine the whole wheat flour, rolled oats, and ground cinnamon (if using).
2. **Add the Wet Ingredients:**
   - Stir in the applesauce or mashed banana, peanut butter, egg, and water or broth. Mix until a firm dough forms. If the dough is too dry, add water 1 tablespoon at a time.
3. **Knead the Dough:**
   - Turn the dough out onto a lightly floured surface and knead it until smooth, about 2-3 minutes.

Step 2: Shape the Biscuits

1. **Roll Out the Dough:**
    ◦ Roll the dough to about ¼-inch thickness using a rolling pin.
2. **Cut Out Shapes:**
    ◦ Use bone-shaped cookie cutters, or for a *Doctor Who* twist, freehand or use a K-9-shaped template to cut out the biscuits with a knife.
3. **Place on Baking Sheet:**
    ◦ Arrange the shapes on a parchment-lined baking sheet, spacing them about 1 inch apart.

Step 3: Bake the Biscuits

1. **Preheat the Oven:**
    ◦ Preheat your oven to 325°F (165°C).
2. **Bake:**
    ◦ Bake the biscuits for 20-25 minutes, or until golden brown and firm. For a crunchier texture, turn off the oven and let the biscuits cool inside with the door slightly ajar.

Decorating K-9 Replicas
Step 1: Prepare Dog-Safe Icing (Optional)

- **Ingredients for Dog-Safe Icing:**
    - ¼ cup plain Greek yogurt
    - 2 tbsp cornstarch
    - 1 tsp beet powder (for red accents)
- **Mix the Icing:**
    - Combine the Greek yogurt and cornstarch to create a thick, pipeable icing. Divide into portions and add beet powder to one portion for a red color.

Step 2: Decorate the Biscuits

1. **Base Coat:**
    - Spread or pipe the plain yogurt icing onto the biscuits for a sleek, robotic look.
2. **Add Details:**
    - Use a toothpick or piping bag with the red icing to add K-9's signature collar or any other accents.
3. **Personal Touch:**
    - If you're feeling extra creative, pipe on K-9's control panel using dog-safe food coloring or carob powder mixed with water for darker details.

Tips for Perfect Canine Crunchers

- **Ingredient Safety:** Always check that the peanut butter is free of xylitol, which is toxic to dogs.
- **Storage:** Store the cookies in an airtight container for up to 1 week at room temperature or 2 weeks in the refrigerator.
- **Custom Shapes:** Use small circular cutters to make mini biscuits for smaller dogs or as training treats.

Bonus: Customization for Cats
If you have feline companions, you can modify this recipe by replacing the applesauce and peanut butter with:

- ½ cup pureed tuna or salmon
- 1 tbsp catnip (optional)

Follow the same steps to create feline-friendly treats!

Serving and Presentation Ideas

- **Doggie Party:** Serve the K-9 Canine Crunchers at a dog-friendly event or as a gift for fellow pet owners.
- **Themed Packaging:** Wrap the biscuits in a TARDIS-blue box for a *Doctor Who*-themed pet treat.
- **Interactive Feeding:** Hide the treats in puzzle toys or training games for mental stimulation.

The Whovian Experience

K-9 Canine Crunchers are more than just treats—they're a celebration of the companionship and loyalty that pets bring to our lives. With their wholesome ingredients, fun shapes, and optional decorations, these biscuits honor the spirit of K-9 while delighting your furry friend.

So, whether you're rewarding good behavior or just showing some love, these treats are sure to earn a tail wag or two. As K-9 would say: **"Affirmative!"**

Allons-y!

Chapter 19: Christmas Crackers of the Shadow Proclamation

Inspired by the Shadow Proclamation, the intergalactic treaty body from *Doctor Who*, these savory Christmas crackers are a nod to the grandeur and sophistication of galactic diplomacy. Infused with bold and unique flavors, these crackers are the perfect addition to any holiday spread. Designed to pair beautifully with festive cheeses and dips, these crackers will elevate your holiday entertaining while paying tribute to the interstellar elegance of the *Doctor Who* universe.

The Concept: Galactic Savory Elegance

The Shadow Proclamation represents unity and balance across the galaxy, and these crackers reflect that ethos with their perfectly balanced flavors and textures. Infused with intergalactic inspiration, each cracker offers a bite of adventure, making them an ideal centerpiece for festive gatherings. Whether enjoyed on their own or paired with rich cheeses and flavorful dips, these crackers are versatile, sophisticated, and delightfully unique.

Ingredients for Christmas Crackers of the Shadow Proclamation

For the Base Cracker Dough (Makes ~40 Crackers):

- 1 ½ cups all-purpose flour (or a mix of all-purpose and whole wheat flour for added texture)
- ½ cup grated Parmesan cheese (or nutritional yeast for a vegan option)
- ½ tsp salt
- ½ tsp black pepper
- ½ tsp smoked paprika
- ¼ tsp ground cumin (optional, for a warm, earthy note)
- 4 tbsp unsalted butter or olive oil
- 6-8 tbsp cold water

For Intergalactic Flavor Variations:

- **Herb & Garlic:** Add 1 tsp dried rosemary, 1 tsp dried thyme, and ½ tsp garlic powder to the dough.
- **Spicy Stardust:** Add ½ tsp red pepper flakes and a pinch of cayenne for heat.
- **Cheesy Nebula:** Add ¼ cup grated sharp cheddar or Gruyère to the dough for a richer flavor.

Instructions: Crafting Christmas Crackers
Step 1: Prepare the Dough

1. **Mix Dry Ingredients:**
    ◦ In a large mixing bowl, whisk together the flour, Parmesan cheese (or nutritional yeast), salt, black pepper, smoked paprika, and cumin (if using).
2. **Incorporate Butter or Oil:**
    ◦ Add the butter or olive oil to the dry ingredients. Use a pastry cutter, fork, or your fingers to blend until the mixture resembles coarse crumbs.
3. **Add Water Gradually:**
    ◦ Stir in the cold water, 1 tablespoon at a time, mixing just until the dough comes together. Be careful not to overwork the dough.

Step 2: Roll Out and Cut the Crackers

1. **Roll the Dough:**
    ◦ Divide the dough into two portions. Roll out one portion on a lightly floured surface to about ⅛-inch thickness.
2. **Cut the Crackers:**
    ◦ Use a sharp knife or cookie cutters to cut the dough into desired shapes (e.g., squares, circles, or festive stars). Transfer the crackers to a parchment-lined baking sheet.
3. **Poke Holes for Texture:**
    ◦ Use a fork to prick holes in the crackers to prevent puffing during baking.

Step 3: Bake the Crackers

1. **Preheat the Oven:**
    ◦ Preheat your oven to 375°F (190°C).
2. **Bake Until Crisp:**
    ◦ Bake the crackers for 10-12 minutes, or until golden brown and crisp. Keep an eye on them, as thinner crackers may bake faster.
3. **Cool Completely:**
    ◦ Transfer the crackers to a wire rack to cool completely. They will crisp up further as they cool.

Pairing Suggestions: Festive Cheeses and Dips

These crackers shine brightest when paired with complementary flavors. Here are some suggestions for creating an intergalactic cheese and dip platter:

Cheese Pairings:

- **Soft Cheeses:** Brie, Camembert, or goat cheese with a drizzle of honey or fig jam.
- **Aged Cheeses:** Sharp cheddar, Parmesan, or Gruyère for bold, nutty flavors.
- **Blue Cheeses:** Gorgonzola or Stilton paired with a sweet chutney or dried fruits.

Dip Pairings:

- **Galactic Hummus:** Classic hummus with a swirl of beet or roasted red pepper puree for a cosmic effect.
- **Spiced Labneh:** Creamy labneh topped with olive oil, za'atar, and pomegranate seeds.
- **Earthy Tapenade:** Olive tapenade or sun-dried tomato spread for a savory punch.

Optional Additions: Garnishes and Flavors

- **Cosmic Seeds:** Sprinkle sesame seeds, poppy seeds, or flaxseeds over the dough before baking for added texture and flavor.
- **Herb Dusting:** Lightly brush the crackers with olive oil and sprinkle with fresh herbs like thyme or rosemary after baking.
- **Edible Glitter:** Dust the crackers with edible silver glitter for a celestial touch that echoes the grandeur of the Shadow Proclamation.

Tips for Perfect Crackers

- **Uniform Thickness:** Roll the dough evenly to ensure consistent baking. Thicker crackers will be softer, while thinner ones will be crispier.
- **Storage:** Store the crackers in an airtight container at room temperature for up to 1 week.
- **Batch Baking:** If making multiple batches, keep unused dough covered to prevent it from drying out.

Serving and Presentation Ideas

- **Galactic Cheese Board:** Arrange the crackers on a platter with cheeses, dips, fresh fruit, and nuts. Add star-shaped crackers for a festive touch.
- **Shadow Proclamation Display:** Use dark serving trays or slate boards with metallic accents to evoke the Shadow Proclamation's mysterious aesthetic.
- **Themed Wrapping:** Package the crackers in TARDIS-blue bags or boxes as edible gifts for *Doctor Who* fans.

The Whovian Experience

Christmas Crackers of the Shadow Proclamation are a culinary journey across the galaxy, combining sophistication, flavor, and a touch of whimsy. These crackers, with their bold spices and customizable flavors, are the perfect companion for your holiday entertaining, bringing the grandeur of intergalactic diplomacy to your table.

Whether served with a lavish cheese board or enjoyed on their own, these crackers are sure to leave a lasting impression—much like the Shadow Proclamation itself. So, gather your companions, assemble your feast, and enjoy a taste of diplomacy that spans the stars.

Allons-y!

Chapter 20: Torchwood Tiramisu

Torchwood, the covert organization tasked with defending Earth from extraterrestrial threats in *Doctor Who*, inspires this rich and indulgent dessert. Much like Torchwood's layered and mysterious nature, this tiramisu features luscious mascarpone cream and coffee-soaked ladyfingers, each layer building a deeper flavor profile. For a festive twist, you can infuse it with peppermint or eggnog flavors, making it perfect for holiday gatherings or *Doctor Who*-themed celebrations.

The Concept: A Dessert of Depth and Mystery

Torchwood Tiramisu combines tradition with innovation, honoring the classic Italian dessert while adding a holiday spin. Its creamy, coffee-infused layers mirror Torchwood's blend of mystery and sophistication, and the optional peppermint or eggnog enhancements bring a festive warmth to this indulgent treat.

Ingredients for Torchwood Tiramisu

Classic Tiramisu Base (Serves 8-10):

- 1 cup strong brewed coffee or espresso, cooled
- 3 tbsp coffee liqueur (optional, such as Kahlúa or Tia Maria)
- 3 large egg yolks
- ½ cup granulated sugar
- 1 cup mascarpone cheese, softened
- 1 cup heavy cream, cold
- 1 tsp vanilla extract
- 1 package ladyfingers (savoiardi)

Holiday Variations:

- **Peppermint Twist:** Add 1 tsp peppermint extract to the mascarpone mixture. Garnish with crushed candy canes.
- **Eggnog Infusion:** Replace the heavy cream with 1 cup eggnog, and add ½ tsp nutmeg to the mascarpone mixture.

For the Topping:

- Unsweetened cocoa powder (for dusting)
- Dark chocolate shavings or curls
- Crushed candy canes or edible glitter for decoration (optional)

Instructions: Crafting Torchwood Tiramisu
Step 1: Prepare the Coffee Mixture

1. **Brew the Coffee:**
    ◦ Brew 1 cup of strong coffee or espresso and let it cool to room temperature. Stir in the coffee liqueur if using.
2. **Prepare for Assembly:**
    ◦ Pour the coffee mixture into a shallow dish wide enough to dip the ladyfingers.

Step 2: Make the Mascarpone Cream

1. **Whisk the Egg Yolks and Sugar:**
    ◦ In a heatproof bowl, whisk the egg yolks and granulated sugar together until smooth. Place the bowl over a pot of simmering water (double boiler) and whisk constantly for 5-7 minutes, or until the mixture thickens slightly and turns pale. Remove from heat and let cool.
2. **Incorporate the Mascarpone:**
    ◦ Gently fold the softened mascarpone into the cooled egg yolk mixture until smooth.
3. **Whip the Cream:**
    ◦ In a separate bowl, whip the heavy cream (or eggnog for the holiday variation) with the vanilla extract until soft peaks form. If making the peppermint variation, add the peppermint extract at this stage.
4. **Combine:**
    ◦ Fold the whipped cream into the mascarpone mixture in two additions, being careful not to deflate the cream.

Step 3: Assemble the Tiramisu

1. **Layer the Ladyfingers:**
    ◦ Quickly dip each ladyfinger into the coffee mixture, ensuring it's fully coated but not soggy. Arrange a single layer of dipped ladyfingers in the bottom of a 9x9-inch dish or trifle bowl.
2. **Spread the Mascarpone Cream:**
    ◦ Spread half of the mascarpone mixture evenly over the layer of ladyfingers.
3. **Repeat:**
    ◦ Add another layer of dipped ladyfingers, followed by the remaining mascarpone cream. Smooth the top with a spatula.

4. **Chill:**
   - Cover the dish with plastic wrap and refrigerate for at least 6 hours, preferably overnight, to allow the flavors to meld and the texture to set.

Step 4: Decorate the Tiramisu

1. **Dust with Cocoa Powder:**
   - Just before serving, dust the top of the tiramisu generously with unsweetened cocoa powder.
2. **Add Garnishes:**
   - For a classic look, sprinkle with dark chocolate shavings or curls. For the holiday variations, add crushed candy canes (peppermint) or a light dusting of nutmeg and edible glitter (eggnog).

Tips for Perfect Torchwood Tiramisu

- **Quality Coffee:** Use high-quality coffee or espresso for the best flavor. If using instant coffee, make it strong and bold.
- **Softening Ladyfingers:** Dip the ladyfingers quickly to prevent them from becoming too soggy and falling apart.
- **Chilling Time:** Allow ample chilling time for the flavors to meld and the layers to set properly.
- **Substitute for Raw Eggs:** If concerned about using raw eggs, use pasteurized eggs or replace the egg yolks with 1 cup of whipped cream folded directly into the mascarpone.

Serving and Presentation Ideas

- **Torchwood Theme:** Serve the tiramisu in a dark dish with subtle metallic accents to evoke Torchwood's sleek aesthetic.
- **Individual Portions:** Use clear glasses or ramekins to create individual servings, showcasing the layers for a dramatic effect.
- **Holiday Platter:** Present the tiramisu on a platter surrounded by festive decorations, such as pine sprigs, fairy lights, or small ornaments.

Holiday Pairings

- **Beverages:** Serve with a cup of espresso, a festive peppermint mocha, or a glass of spiked eggnog.
- **Light Accompaniments:** Pair with crisp biscotti or almond cookies for a complementary texture.

The Whovian Experience

Torchwood Tiramisu is a dessert that combines richness, sophistication, and a touch of intrigue. Its layers of coffee-soaked ladyfingers and mascarpone cream are as mysterious and complex as the Torchwood Institute itself, while the holiday variations bring a festive cheer to this timeless classic.

As you savor each luxurious bite, let the flavors transport you to the world of Torchwood, where decadence meets adventure in every layer.

Allons-y!

Chapter 21: Alien Antipasto Platters

An antipasto platter is a feast for the senses, offering a variety of flavors, textures, and colors that excite the palate. In this chapter, we take the classic antipasto to the stars with an intergalactic twist. Combining bold ingredients, creative arrangements, and unique homemade recipes, these Alien Antipasto Platters are sure to impress guests at your next gathering. With recipes for pickles, marinated olives, and charcuterie pairings, you'll learn how to create a platter that feels like it's been served at a cosmic cantina.

The Concept: An Intergalactic Feast of Flavors

Antipasto platters traditionally serve as a prelude to a meal, offering a harmonious blend of savory, salty, and tangy bites. Inspired by the infinite diversity of the universe, this platter incorporates unique flavors, celestial arrangements, and a touch of *Doctor Who*-inspired whimsy. From vibrant marinated olives to cosmic charcuterie combinations, this antipasto platter invites your guests to explore new tastes while celebrating the art of presentation.

Building Your Alien Antipasto Platter
Essential Components

1. **Cured Meats:** A variety of charcuterie items provide a savory backbone.
2. **Cheeses:** Offer an assortment of textures and flavors, from creamy to aged.
3. **Pickled Items:** Add tangy brightness with homemade pickles or pickled vegetables.
4. **Marinated Olives:** Bold and briny olives bring a Mediterranean flair.
5. **Fresh Elements:** Include fresh fruits, vegetables, and herbs for balance.
6. **Crunchy Additions:** Provide crackers, breadsticks, or crostini for texture.
7. **Dips and Spreads:** Offer complementary flavors like hummus, pesto, or roasted pepper dip.

Recipes for Key Components
1. Homemade Pickles: Cosmic Cucumber Spears

- **Ingredients:**
    - 4 small cucumbers, quartered into spears
    - 1 cup white vinegar
    - 1 cup water
    - 2 tbsp sugar
    - 1 tbsp salt
    - 1 tsp mustard seeds
    - 1 tsp dill seeds
    - 2 garlic cloves, smashed
    - 1 sprig fresh dill

- **Instructions:**
    - Combine the vinegar, water, sugar, and salt in a saucepan. Heat until the sugar and salt dissolve. Let cool slightly.
    - Place the cucumber spears, mustard seeds, dill seeds, garlic, and fresh dill into a clean jar.
    - Pour the brine over the cucumbers, ensuring they are fully submerged.
    - Seal the jar and refrigerate for at least 24 hours. These pickles can be stored for up to 2 weeks.

2. Marinated Olives: Galactic Olive Mix

- **Ingredients:**
    - 2 cups mixed olives (green, black, and Kalamata)
    - 3 tbsp olive oil
    - 1 tbsp red wine vinegar
    - 2 garlic cloves, thinly sliced
    - 1 tsp dried oregano
    - ½ tsp red pepper flakes
    - Zest of 1 lemon
    - Fresh rosemary and thyme sprigs
- **Instructions:**
    - In a mixing bowl, combine olive oil, vinegar, garlic, oregano, red pepper flakes, and lemon zest.
    - Add the olives and toss to coat. Mix in fresh rosemary and thyme.
    - Let the olives marinate in the refrigerator for at least 2 hours, preferably overnight, for maximum flavor.

3. Charcuterie: Planetary Pairings

- **Suggested Meats:**
    - **Prosciutto:** Silky and savory, perfect for wrapping around fresh fruit like melon.
    - **Salami:** Bold and spiced, offering a hearty bite.
    - **Capicola:** Smoky and rich, a great balance to lighter cheeses.
- **Pairing Tips:**
    - Arrange meats in "rivers" or spiral patterns for a celestial appearance.
    - Roll or fold slices to create visual interest and maximize platter space.

Cheese Suggestions

1. **Creamy Cheeses:** Brie, Camembert, or Burrata
   - Serve with honey or fruit preserves for sweetness.
2. **Aged Cheeses:** Parmesan, Manchego, or Gouda
   - Pair with marinated olives or roasted nuts.
3. **Blue Cheeses:** Gorgonzola or Roquefort
   - Complement with fresh figs or a drizzle of balsamic glaze.

Fresh Elements: A Breath of Earth

1. **Fruits:**
   - Grapes, sliced apples, or fresh figs provide natural sweetness.
   - Add pomegranate seeds for a burst of color and tang.
2. **Vegetables:**
   - Include cherry tomatoes, bell pepper strips, or radishes for crunch.
   - Arrange cucumber slices into overlapping circles to resemble alien patterns.
3. **Herbs:**
   - Scatter fresh rosemary, thyme, or edible flowers to enhance the visual appeal.

Crunchy Additions: Galactic Grains

1. **Crostini:** Toast thin slices of baguette and rub with garlic for extra flavor.
2. **Breadsticks:** Add a whimsical touch by wrapping breadsticks with prosciutto.
3. **Crackers:** Offer a variety of textures, from seeded crackers to buttery wafers.

Dips and Spreads

1. **Hummus with a Twist:**
   - Swirl in beet puree for a vibrant magenta color.
2. **Roasted Red Pepper Dip:**
   - Blend roasted red peppers, olive oil, garlic, and almonds for a smoky, tangy spread.
3. **Pesto:**
   - Use traditional basil pesto or experiment with arugula or sun-dried tomato varieties.

Assembling Your Alien Antipasto Platter

1. **Start with Larger Items:**
   ◦ Begin with cheeses and dips, placing them in small bowls or clusters around the platter.
2. **Add Meats and Pickles:**
   ◦ Arrange cured meats in spirals or fans, and place pickles in small jars or bowls.
3. **Incorporate Olives and Fresh Elements:**
   ◦ Fill in gaps with marinated olives, fresh fruits, and vegetables.
4. **Finish with Crackers and Garnishes:**
   ◦ Tuck crackers and breadsticks into empty spaces, and scatter herbs and edible flowers for decoration.

Tips for a Cosmic Presentation

- **Use Levels:** Create dimension by using bowls, small stands, or overturned ramekins to elevate certain elements.
- **Color Balance:** Distribute colors evenly to create visual harmony.
- **Celestial Touches:** Add star-shaped crackers or sprinkle edible glitter for a galactic effect.

Pairing Ideas for Drinks

- **Wine:** Pair with a crisp Sauvignon Blanc, a fruity Pinot Noir, or a bold Cabernet Sauvignon.
- **Mocktails:** Serve with sparkling water infused with citrus and fresh herbs for a refreshing, non-alcoholic option.
- **Cocktails:** A Negroni or an Aperol Spritz complements the flavors beautifully.

The Whovian Experience

An Alien Antipasto Platter is more than just an appetizer—it's a feast for the eyes and the palate, inspired by the rich diversity of the universe. With its bold flavors, creative presentation, and nods to the *Doctor Who* universe, this platter is a celebration of culinary exploration.

Whether you're hosting a festive gathering or a *Doctor Who*-themed party, this antipasto platter invites your guests to embark on a journey of flavor and creativity.

Allons-y!

Chapter 22: The Doctor's All-Time All-Bran Muffins

The Doctor's All-Time All-Bran Muffins are the perfect antidote to holiday indulgence, offering a health-conscious, nutrient-packed treat that doesn't skimp on flavor. Inspired by the Doctor's love of balance and creativity, these muffins combine the goodness of bran with a medley of "Gallifreyan" fruits and nuts—earthly superfoods that evoke an intergalactic twist. Whether you're looking for a quick breakfast, a post-holiday detox snack, or a healthier dessert option, these muffins will have you ready to face any timey-wimey adventure.

The Concept: Healthy Meets Flavorful

While the holidays are a time for indulgence, these All-Bran muffins are here to bring balance back to your plate. They are high in fiber, packed with essential nutrients, and sweetened naturally with fruits and honey. Each bite offers a delightful mix of textures and flavors, from the crunch of nuts to the chewiness of dried fruits, creating a muffin that's as delicious as it is nourishing.

Ingredients for The Doctor's All-Time All-Bran Muffins
Dry Ingredients:

- 1 ½ cups wheat bran
- 1 cup whole wheat flour
- 1 tsp baking powder
- 1 tsp baking soda
- ½ tsp salt
- 1 tsp ground cinnamon
- ½ tsp ground nutmeg

Wet Ingredients:

- ½ cup honey or maple syrup
- ⅓ cup vegetable oil or melted coconut oil
- 2 large eggs
- 1 cup buttermilk or plain yogurt (for a dairy-free option, use almond milk with 1 tsp vinegar)
- 1 tsp vanilla extract

Gallifreyan Fruits and Nuts:

- ½ cup chopped dried apricots (Gallifreyan "sunberries")
- ½ cup raisins or dried cranberries (Gallifreyan "star clusters")
- ½ cup chopped walnuts or almonds (Gallifreyan "nebula nuts")
- 2 tbsp chia seeds or flaxseeds (optional, for added fiber and omega-3s)

Instructions: Crafting All-Time All-Bran Muffins
Step 1: Prepare the Dry Ingredients

1. **Mix the Base:**
   - In a large mixing bowl, combine the wheat bran, whole wheat flour, baking powder, baking soda, salt, cinnamon, and nutmeg. Whisk until evenly distributed.

Step 2: Prepare the Wet Ingredients

1. **Combine the Liquids:**
   - In a separate bowl, whisk together the honey (or maple syrup), oil, eggs, buttermilk (or yogurt), and vanilla extract until smooth.

Step 3: Combine the Wet and Dry Ingredients

1. **Mix the Batter:**
   - Gradually pour the wet ingredients into the dry ingredients, stirring gently with a wooden spoon or spatula until just combined. Do not overmix; the batter should be slightly lumpy.
2. **Fold in the Fruits and Nuts:**
   - Add the chopped dried apricots, raisins, walnuts, and chia seeds (if using). Fold them gently into the batter until evenly distributed.

Step 4: Bake the Muffins

1. **Preheat the Oven:**
   - Preheat your oven to 375°F (190°C). Line a 12-cup muffin tin with paper liners or grease the cups lightly.
2. **Fill the Muffin Cups:**
   - Spoon the batter evenly into the prepared muffin cups, filling each about three-quarters full.
3. **Bake:**
   - Bake the muffins for 18-22 minutes, or until a toothpick inserted into the center comes out clean.
4. **Cool:**
   - Let the muffins cool in the pan for 5 minutes, then transfer them to a wire rack to cool completely.

Optional Variations

1. **Chocolate Boost:**
   - Add ¼ cup dark chocolate chips for a touch of indulgence.
2. **Citrus Twist:**
   - Fold in 1 tbsp grated orange or lemon zest for a refreshing zing.
3. **Berry Explosion:**
   - Replace dried fruits with fresh or frozen berries for a juicier texture.
4. **Vegan Muffins:**
   - Replace eggs with flax eggs (1 tbsp ground flaxseed mixed with 3 tbsp water per egg) and use a plant-based milk alternative.

Nutritional Benefits of the Doctor's All-Bran Muffins

1. **High in Fiber:**
   - The wheat bran, whole wheat flour, and dried fruits provide ample dietary fiber to support digestive health.
2. **Rich in Healthy Fats:**
   - Nuts and seeds contribute heart-healthy fats and essential nutrients like omega-3s.
3. **Natural Sweetness:**
   - Sweetened with honey or maple syrup, these muffins avoid refined sugar.
4. **Protein-Packed:**
   - The eggs, nuts, and seeds add protein, making these muffins a satisfying snack or breakfast option.

Serving and Storage Tips

1. **Serving Suggestions:**
   - Enjoy warm with a dollop of Greek yogurt and a drizzle of honey.
   - Pair with a hot cup of tea or coffee for a cozy breakfast.
2. **Storage:**
   - Store muffins in an airtight container at room temperature for up to 3 days, or refrigerate for up to 1 week. For longer storage, freeze individually wrapped muffins for up to 3 months.
3. **Reheating:**
   - Reheat frozen muffins in the microwave for 20-30 seconds or in a 350°F (175°C) oven for 5-7 minutes.

The Doctor's Whovian Inspiration

The Doctor's All-Time All-Bran Muffins are inspired by the Time Lord's commitment to balance and resilience. Each ingredient is chosen to support energy, health, and vitality, mirroring the Doctor's boundless energy and enthusiasm for life. With their rich flavors and nutrient-packed profile, these muffins are a testament to the idea that healthy eating can be exciting, delicious, and endlessly creative.

The Whovian Experience

As you enjoy these muffins, imagine the Doctor sharing them with companions in the TARDIS, fueling adventures through time and space. With their hearty ingredients and intergalactic flair, these All-Bran muffins bring a touch of *Doctor Who* magic to your kitchen, ensuring you're ready to take on whatever the universe throws your way.

Allons-y!

Chapter 23: Jelly Baby Jellies

Few treats are as synonymous with *Doctor Who* as the Doctor's iconic jelly babies. These playful, chewy sweets have become a symbol of the Doctor's charm, wit, and penchant for unexpected kindness. In this chapter, we recreate the magic of jelly babies with a homemade twist. Learn how to craft your own jelly candies in a variety of colors and flavors, customizing them to suit any occasion while staying true to their whimsical origins.

The Concept: Nostalgia Meets Creativity

Jelly Baby Jellies are more than just sweets—they're a tribute to the Doctor's legacy and an invitation to relive the joy and playfulness they bring to every scene they appear in. These homemade candies are easy to make, completely customizable, and far more flavorful than their store-bought counterparts. Plus, their vibrant colors and fruity flavors make them a delightful treat for fans of all ages.

Ingredients for Jelly Baby Jellies
Base Jelly Candy Mixture (Yields ~30 candies):

- 1 cup fruit juice (choose from orange, apple, grape, or cranberry for natural colors and flavors)
- 2 tbsp unflavored gelatin (or agar-agar for a vegan alternative)
- ⅓ cup granulated sugar (adjust based on sweetness of juice)
- 1 tbsp honey or light corn syrup (for a smoother texture)
- 1 tsp lemon juice (optional, for a tangy kick)
- Gel food coloring (optional, for more vibrant hues)

Equipment Needed

- Silicone jelly baby molds (or other fun candy molds)
- Small saucepan
- Whisk
- Dropper or small spoon for pouring mixture into molds
- Parchment paper for setting candies

Instructions: Crafting Jelly Baby Jellies
Step 1: Prepare the Ingredients

1. **Choose Your Juice:**
    - Select a fruit juice as the base. Opt for natural, clear juices to ensure a smooth texture and vibrant color.
2. **Gather Supplies:**
    - Set up your candy molds on a baking tray for stability. Lightly grease the molds with a neutral oil to ensure easy release.

Step 2: Make the Jelly Mixture

1. **Heat the Juice:**
    - In a small saucepan, combine the fruit juice, sugar, and honey (or corn syrup). Heat over medium-low, stirring until the sugar dissolves. Do not let the mixture boil.
2. **Dissolve the Gelatin or Agar-Agar:**
    - Gradually sprinkle the gelatin (or agar-agar) into the warm juice, whisking continuously to prevent clumps. Continue stirring over low heat until fully dissolved, about 3-5 minutes.
3. **Add Lemon Juice and Coloring:**
    - Stir in the lemon juice for brightness, and add gel food coloring if desired to enhance the hue of the candies.

Step 3: Fill the Molds

1. **Pour the Mixture:**
    - Use a dropper or small spoon to carefully fill the jelly baby molds with the warm mixture. Tap the mold tray gently on the counter to remove air bubbles.
2. **Chill to Set:**
    - Transfer the molds to the refrigerator and chill for at least 2 hours, or until the jellies are firm and set.

Step 4: Release and Finish

1. **Remove from Molds:**
    - Once set, gently pop the jelly candies out of the molds. Use clean, dry hands to handle them.
2. **Optional Coating:**
    - For a classic jelly baby finish, roll the candies lightly in granulated sugar.

Customizing Colors and Flavors
Color Variations:

- **Red:** Use cherry, pomegranate, or cranberry juice; add a few drops of red food coloring if needed.
- **Orange:** Use orange or mango juice for a sunny hue.
- **Yellow:** Try pineapple or lemon juice, adding a pinch of turmeric for a natural yellow tint.
- **Green:** Blend apple juice with spinach extract or green food coloring for a subtle green shade.
- **Purple:** Use grape or blueberry juice for a rich, deep color.

Flavor Enhancements:

- Add a few drops of fruit extracts (like raspberry, orange, or lime) to intensify flavors.
- Mix in spices like cinnamon or ginger for a festive twist.
- Infuse the juice with fresh herbs like mint or basil for a sophisticated flavor profile.

Tips for Perfect Jelly Baby Jellies

1. **Control Sweetness:**
   - Taste your juice before adding sugar. Adjust sweetness based on the natural sugar content of the juice.
2. **Work Quickly:**
   - The gelatin mixture sets quickly, so have your molds ready before you start heating the juice.
3. **Storage:**
   - Store jellies in an airtight container in the refrigerator for up to 1 week. Separate layers with parchment paper to prevent sticking.
4. **Vegan Substitution:**
   - When using agar-agar, adjust the amount to 1 tbsp for every 2 tbsp of gelatin, and bring the mixture to a boil before simmering for 1-2 minutes.

Serving and Presentation Ideas

- **Themed Packaging:**
  - Wrap the jelly babies in small cellophane bags tied with TARDIS-blue ribbon for party favors or gifts.
- **Whovian Display:**
  - Arrange the jelly babies in a bowl with a tiny TARDIS figurine nestled among them.
- **Festive Additions:**
  - Mix jelly babies with other sweets like licorice or chocolate coins for a fun holiday candy platter.

The Whovian Experience

Jelly Baby Jellies are a playful nod to the Doctor's timeless charm, bringing a taste of intergalactic whimsy to your kitchen. Whether you enjoy them as a nostalgic treat or share them with fellow fans, these homemade candies capture the spirit of *Doctor Who*—quirky, colorful, and unforgettable.

As you savor each chewy, fruity bite, remember: "Would you like a jelly baby?"

Allons-y!

Chapter 24: Planetary Pastries

From the scarred landscapes of Skaro to the shimmering beauty of Gallifrey, the *Doctor Who* universe is rich with iconic planets. In this chapter, we bring the wonders of these celestial bodies to life with mini pies and pastries inspired by their unique aesthetics and flavors. The recipes for "Skaro Strawberry Tarts" and "Gallifreyan Galaxy Pies" are designed to evoke the essence of these legendary worlds, blending creativity with indulgence in every bite.

The Concept: Baking Across the Universe

Planetary Pastries are a delicious way to explore the *Doctor Who* universe through your taste buds. Each pastry is carefully crafted to reflect the essence of its namesake planet, from the dark and mysterious Skaro to the golden grandeur of Gallifrey. These mini treats are perfect for parties, themed events, or simply indulging your love for *Doctor Who*.

Recipe 1: Skaro Strawberry Tarts

Skaro, home of the Daleks, inspires these bold and dramatic tarts. The deep red strawberry filling symbolizes the planet's scarred surface, while a dark chocolate drizzle nods to the Daleks' menacing presence.

Ingredients for Skaro Strawberry Tarts (Makes 6 Mini Tarts):

For the Tart Shells:

- 1 ½ cups all-purpose flour
- ½ cup unsalted butter, cold and cubed
- 3 tbsp granulated sugar
- 1 egg yolk
- 2-3 tbsp ice water

For the Strawberry Filling:

- 2 cups fresh or frozen strawberries, hulled and chopped
- ⅓ cup granulated sugar
- 1 tbsp cornstarch mixed with 2 tbsp water
- 1 tsp lemon juice

For the Decoration:

- 3 oz dark chocolate, melted
- Edible silver stars or metallic sprinkles (optional, for a cosmic touch)

Instructions:
Step 1: Make the Tart Shells

1. **Prepare the Dough:**
   - In a large bowl, mix the flour and sugar. Add the cold butter and use a pastry cutter or your fingers to rub the butter into the flour until the mixture resembles coarse crumbs.
   - Add the egg yolk and ice water, 1 tablespoon at a time, mixing until the dough comes together. Form into a disk, wrap in plastic wrap, and chill for 30 minutes.
2. **Roll and Bake:**
   - Preheat your oven to 375°F (190°C). Roll out the dough to ⅛-inch thickness on a lightly floured surface. Cut out circles slightly larger than your tart pans and press them into the pans.
   - Prick the bottoms with a fork and bake for 12-15 minutes, or until golden brown. Cool completely.

Step 2: Prepare the Strawberry Filling

1. **Cook the Filling:**
   - In a medium saucepan, combine the strawberries, sugar, and lemon juice. Cook over medium heat until the strawberries soften and release their juices.
   - Stir in the cornstarch slurry and cook until the mixture thickens. Let cool to room temperature.
2. **Assemble the Tarts:**
   - Spoon the strawberry filling into the cooled tart shells.

Step 3: Decorate the Tarts

1. **Add the Chocolate Drizzle:**
   - Use a spoon or piping bag to drizzle melted dark chocolate over the tarts in bold, jagged lines reminiscent of Skaro's harsh terrain.
2. **Finish with Cosmic Flair:**
   - Sprinkle edible silver stars or metallic sprinkles for a galactic touch.

Recipe 2: Gallifreyan Galaxy Pies

Gallifrey, the Doctor's home planet, inspires these elegant mini pies. Their golden crusts represent Gallifrey's twin suns, while a swirling blueberry filling evokes the mysterious time vortex.

Ingredients for Gallifreyan Galaxy Pies (Makes 6 Mini Pies):

For the Pie Crust:

- 1 ½ cups all-purpose flour
- ½ cup unsalted butter, cold and cubed
- ¼ tsp salt
- 2-3 tbsp ice water

For the Blueberry Filling:

- 2 cups fresh or frozen blueberries
- ¼ cup granulated sugar
- 1 tbsp cornstarch mixed with 2 tbsp water
- 1 tsp vanilla extract
- ½ tsp cinnamon (optional)

For the Swirl Effect:

- ¼ cup raspberry or cherry jam, warmed and strained

For the Decoration:

- Edible gold luster dust or glitter
- Star-shaped pastry cutouts (optional)

Instructions:
Step 1: Make the Pie Crust

1. **Prepare the Dough:**
   - In a large bowl, mix the flour and salt. Add the cold butter and work it into the flour until the mixture resembles coarse crumbs.
   - Gradually add the ice water, mixing until the dough just comes together. Form into a disk, wrap in plastic wrap, and chill for 30 minutes.
2. **Roll and Cut:**
   - Preheat your oven to 375°F (190°C). Roll out the dough to ⅛-inch thickness and cut out circles large enough to fit into a muffin tin. Gently press the circles into the greased muffin cups.

Step 2: Prepare the Blueberry Filling

1. **Cook the Filling:**
   - In a saucepan, combine the blueberries, sugar, vanilla extract, and cinnamon. Cook over medium heat until the berries release their juices.
   - Stir in the cornstarch slurry and cook until thickened. Let cool slightly.
2. **Create the Swirl Effect:**
   - Spoon the blueberry filling into the pie crusts. Drizzle the warmed raspberry jam over the top and use a toothpick to create swirling patterns.

Step 3: Bake and Decorate

1. **Bake the Pies:**
   - Bake for 20-25 minutes, or until the crust is golden brown and the filling is bubbling. Let cool before removing from the muffin tin.
2. **Add the Golden Touch:**
   - Dust the pie crusts lightly with edible gold luster dust to mimic Gallifrey's golden skies.
3. **Starry Accents:**
   - Add small star-shaped pastry cutouts to the top of each pie before baking, or garnish with edible glitter after baking.

Tips for Perfect Planetary Pastries

1. **Chill the Dough:**
    ◦ Keeping the dough cold ensures a flaky crust. If it starts to warm while working, pop it back in the fridge for a few minutes.
2. **Balance Sweetness:**
    ◦ Adjust the sugar in the fillings based on the natural sweetness of your fruits.
3. **Creative Presentation:**
    ◦ Arrange the pastries on a black platter with fairy lights for a celestial-themed display.
4. **Make Ahead:**
    ◦ Both the tart shells and pie crusts can be prepared a day in advance and stored in the refrigerator.

The Whovian Experience

Planetary Pastries transform your kitchen into an intergalactic bakery, capturing the essence of the *Doctor Who* universe in every bite. Whether you're savoring the dramatic flavors of Skaro or the elegant beauty of Gallifrey, these mini pies and tarts are a delicious journey through time and space.

Serve these treats at your next *Doctor Who*-themed party, and let your guests experience the wonders of the universe—one pastry at a time.

Allons-y!

Chapter 25: Regeneration Fruitcake

Fruitcake, often divisive in holiday traditions, receives a *Doctor Who*-inspired transformation in this chapter. The Regeneration Fruitcake begins as a dense, flavorful classic, packed with fruits and nuts, and evolves into a lighter, modern dessert with the addition of frosting layers. This two-in-one dessert mirrors the Doctor's regenerative process, blending tradition with renewal, and offering a sweet treat that appeals to both classic and modern tastes.

The Concept: A Dessert That Regenerates

Like the Doctor, this fruitcake adapts to suit the occasion. It starts as a richly spiced, traditional fruitcake, perfect for those who love the classics. For those seeking something lighter, it "regenerates" into a layered cake with cream cheese frosting and candied fruit accents, breathing new life into the holiday favorite.

Ingredients for Regeneration Fruitcake

For the Base Fruitcake (Makes a 9-inch round cake):

- 2 cups mixed dried fruits (raisins, cranberries, apricots, and cherries)
- ½ cup chopped nuts (walnuts, pecans, or almonds)
- 1 cup all-purpose flour
- ½ tsp baking powder
- ½ tsp baking soda
- ½ tsp salt
- 1 tsp ground cinnamon
- ½ tsp ground nutmeg
- ¼ tsp ground cloves
- ½ cup unsalted butter, softened
- ½ cup brown sugar
- 2 large eggs
- ½ cup molasses or dark honey
- ½ cup orange juice or brewed tea (for soaking fruits)
- Zest of 1 orange
- 1 tsp vanilla extract

For the Frosting and Decoration (Optional for Regeneration Cake):

- 1 cup cream cheese, softened
- ½ cup unsalted butter, softened
- 3 cups powdered sugar, sifted
- 1 tsp vanilla extract
- 1-2 tbsp milk (to adjust consistency)
- Additional dried fruits or candied citrus slices for garnish

Instructions: Crafting the Regeneration Fruitcake
Step 1: Prepare the Fruits and Nuts

1. **Soak the Fruits:**
   ◦ Combine the dried fruits and orange juice (or tea) in a bowl. Let soak for at least 2 hours, or overnight, to plump up the fruits and infuse them with flavor.
2. **Prepare the Nuts:**
   ◦ Lightly toast the nuts in a dry skillet over medium heat for 2-3 minutes to enhance their flavor. Let cool.

Step 2: Mix the Cake Batter

1. **Prepare the Dry Ingredients:**
   ◦ In a medium bowl, whisk together the flour, baking powder, baking soda, salt, cinnamon, nutmeg, and cloves.
2. **Cream the Butter and Sugar:**
   ◦ In a large mixing bowl, beat the softened butter and brown sugar until light and fluffy, about 2-3 minutes.
3. **Add the Wet Ingredients:**
   ◦ Beat in the eggs, one at a time, followed by the molasses, orange zest, and vanilla extract.
4. **Combine the Mixtures:**
   ◦ Gradually add the dry ingredients to the wet mixture, alternating with the soaked fruits (including any remaining liquid). Stir in the toasted nuts until just combined.

Step 3: Bake the Fruitcake

1. **Prepare the Pan:**
   ◦ Preheat your oven to 325°F (165°C). Grease a 9-inch round cake pan and line the bottom with parchment paper.
2. **Bake:**
   ◦ Pour the batter into the prepared pan and smooth the top. Bake for 60-75 minutes, or until a toothpick inserted in the center comes out clean.
3. **Cool:**
   ◦ Let the cake cool in the pan for 10 minutes, then transfer to a wire rack to cool completely.

Regeneration: Transforming the Fruitcake

To "regenerate" your fruitcake into a layered dessert, follow these steps:

Step 1: Slice the Cake

1. **Level the Cake:**
   - Use a serrated knife to level the top of the fruitcake if it has domed during baking.
2. **Create Layers:**
   - Slice the fruitcake horizontally into two or three even layers, depending on your desired thickness.

Step 2: Make the Cream Cheese Frosting

1. **Beat the Cream Cheese and Butter:**
   - In a mixing bowl, beat the cream cheese and butter until smooth and creamy.
2. **Add Powdered Sugar:**
   - Gradually add the powdered sugar, 1 cup at a time, beating well after each addition.
3. **Adjust Consistency:**
   - Stir in the vanilla extract and add milk as needed to achieve a spreadable consistency.

Step 3: Assemble the Regeneration Cake

1. **Frost the Layers:**
   - Place the bottom layer of fruitcake on a serving plate. Spread an even layer of frosting over the top. Repeat with the remaining layers.
2. **Frost the Outside:**
   - Spread a thin crumb coat over the outside of the cake, then apply a final, smooth layer of frosting.
3. **Decorate:**
   - Garnish with additional dried fruits, candied citrus slices, or a dusting of edible glitter for a festive touch.

Tips for Perfect Regeneration Fruitcake

1. **Moisture Matters:**
   - Soaking the fruits is key to keeping the fruitcake moist and flavorful. Don't skip this step.
2. **Aging the Cake:**
   - For a traditional fruitcake experience, wrap the baked cake in cheesecloth soaked with brandy or rum, and store in an airtight container for up to 3 weeks, brushing with more alcohol weekly.
3. **Layer with Precision:**
   - Use a cake leveler or dental floss to ensure even slices for the layered version.
4. **Flavor Enhancements:**
   - Add a pinch of cardamom or allspice for a unique twist, or stir in some chocolate chips for a touch of indulgence.

Serving and Presentation Ideas

1. **Classic Fruitcake:**
   - Serve slices of the fruitcake as-is with a cup of hot tea or mulled wine.
2. **Regenerated Dessert:**
   - Present the layered regeneration cake on a festive cake stand, adorned with holiday greenery or small ornaments.
3. **Mini Versions:**
   - Bake the fruitcake batter in muffin tins to create individual mini fruitcakes, perfect for gifting.

The Whovian Experience

The Regeneration Fruitcake pays homage to the Doctor's ever-changing yet familiar nature. Whether you enjoy it as a traditional holiday fruitcake or a modern layered dessert, this recipe captures the essence of transformation and celebration.

Serve this treat at your next *Doctor Who* marathon or holiday gathering, and let your guests marvel at the magic of a dessert that regenerates into something entirely new.

Allons-y!

Appendices
Appendix A: Gallifreyan Cooking Glossary
Key Spices, Ingredients, and Their Origins in the Whoniverse

The Whoniverse is as rich and diverse as the galaxies it spans, and its culinary traditions reflect this boundless creativity. In this appendix, we explore the key spices, ingredients, and their imaginative origins in the *Doctor Who* universe, offering insights into their uses, flavors, and connections to iconic locations and characters. Use this glossary as a guide to add a touch of intergalactic flair to your cooking.

Key Spices
1. Temporal Thyme

- **Flavor Profile:** Earthy, slightly citrusy, with a hint of mint.
- **Origins:** Said to grow wild in the temporal rifts of Gallifrey's red grass fields. Legend has it that the Time Lords used Temporal Thyme to brew restorative teas.
- **Uses:** Perfect for roasting meats, infusing teas, or adding depth to savory pies.

2. Star Anise Nebulae

- **Flavor Profile:** Sweet, licorice-like, with warm undertones.
- **Origins:** Harvested from the asteroid belts of the Medusa Cascade, these star-shaped spices are a favorite in intergalactic dessert recipes.
- **Uses:** Ideal for spiced cakes, mulled wines, and syrups.

3. Chronon Peppercorns

- **Flavor Profile:** Spicy and bold, with a slight smoky aftertaste.
- **Origins:** Grown in the volcanic soils of Skaro, Chronon Peppercorns are said to possess the sharpness of Dalek logic.
- **Uses:** A must-have for seasoning roasts, stews, and bold marinades.

4. Moonsalt Crystals

- **Flavor Profile:** Subtly mineral and slightly sweet.
- **Origins:** Harvested from the saline seas of the Moon of Poosh, this rare salt is prized for its shimmering, pearlescent grains.
- **Uses:** Enhances the flavor of both sweet and savory dishes, making it perfect for caramel sauces or roasted vegetables.

5. TARDIS Turmeric

- **Flavor Profile:** Warm, earthy, and slightly bitter.
- **Origins:** Believed to have been cultivated on Gallifrey's twin suns, TARDIS Turmeric is said to have time-bending properties when brewed in tea.
- **Uses:** Adds vibrant color and flavor to curries, soups, and golden milk.

Unique Ingredients
1. Red Grass Grain

- **Description:** A hearty, nutty grain native to Gallifrey's plains, often used as a base for breads and porridges.
- **Uses:** Ideal for making rustic bread, pilafs, and as a substitute for rice or quinoa.

2. Vortex Honey

- **Description:** A rare and golden honey produced by the bees of the Time Vortex, rumored to have healing properties.
- **Origins:** Often tied to the disappearance of Earth bees, this honey is prized for its floral complexity.
- **Uses:** Perfect for sweetening teas, drizzling over desserts, or glazing roasted vegetables.

3. Raxacoricofallapatorian Beans

- **Description:** Large, vibrant green beans with a creamy texture and slightly nutty flavor.
- **Origins:** Indigenous to Raxacoricofallapatorius, these beans are a staple in the Slitheen diet.
- **Uses:** Excellent in hearty stews, pureed as a dip, or served sautéed with garlic and olive oil.

4. Shadowberries

- **Description:** Small, jet-black berries with a sweet-tart flavor, thought to grow in the shadowed regions of Trenzalore.
- **Uses:** Used in jams, pies, and syrups; pairs wonderfully with dark chocolate.

5. Gallifreyan Glowfruit

- **Description:** A bioluminescent fruit with a sweet, tropical flavor resembling a mix of pineapple and mango.
- **Origins:** Found only in the hidden orchards of Gallifrey, glowfruit emits a soft golden light when sliced.
- **Uses:** A stunning addition to fruit salads, sorbets, or tropical cocktails.

Infusions and Elixirs
1. Sonic Spice Blend

- **Description:** A mix of Temporal Thyme, Chronon Peppercorns, and TARDIS Turmeric, finely ground for a flavor-packed seasoning.
- **Origins:** Created by Time Lords as a universal seasoning that adapts to the dish it's used in.
- **Uses:** Excellent for grilling, roasting, or sprinkling over popcorn.

2. Dalek Extract

- **Description:** A dark, molasses-like syrup derived from Skaro's native plants, with an intense, smoky sweetness.
- **Origins:** Used by Daleks to enhance energy reserves, this extract has found culinary use as a unique sweetener.
- **Uses:** Ideal for marinades, barbecue sauces, and dark caramel desserts.

3. Omega Oil

- **Description:** A golden oil pressed from the seeds of the Red Grass Grain, with a subtle nutty flavor.
- **Origins:** Named for the infamous Time Lord Omega, this oil is known for its high omega-3 content.
- **Uses:** Perfect for dressings, drizzling over roasted vegetables, or as a finishing oil for soups.

Rare and Exotic Additions
1. Pandorica Petals

- **Description:** Delicate, edible petals with a peppery kick, said to bloom only near temporal fractures.
- **Uses:** A striking garnish for salads, cakes, or savory tarts.

2. Silurian Seaweed Flakes

- **Description:** Dark green, crispy flakes harvested from the subterranean oceans of the Silurian world.
- **Uses:** Adds a savory, umami punch to soups, rice dishes, and seafood recipes.

3. Cyberium Cacao

- **Description:** An intensely dark, bittersweet chocolate believed to have originated from Cyberman colonies.

- **Uses:** Best in ganaches, mousses, or as a rich hot chocolate base.

4. Ice Warrior Mint

- **Description:** A frosty herb with an intense, cooling sensation, native to Mars.
- **Uses:** Great for cocktails, desserts, or as a garnish for iced teas.

Culinary Origins of the Whoniverse

- **Gallifrey:** Known for its refined, herbaceous flavors and time-warping infusions, often centered around Red Grass and Temporal Thyme.
- **Skaro:** Characterized by bold, smoky, and spicy flavors, reflecting its volcanic landscapes.
- **Raxacoricofallapatorius:** Known for vibrant, hearty vegetables like Raxacoricofallapatorian Beans.
- **Trenzalore:** Features dark, sweet ingredients like Shadowberries, reflecting its somber, mysterious nature.
- **The Moon of Poosh:** Famous for its Moonsalt Crystals, adding a luxurious touch to dishes.

This Gallifreyan Cooking Glossary bridges the culinary traditions of Earth and the Whoniverse, infusing your kitchen with the creativity, adventure, and wonder that define *Doctor Who*. Whether you're crafting a Gallifreyan feast or experimenting with Skaro-inspired spices, let this guide serve as your intergalactic culinary companion.

Allons-y!

Appendix B: Substitution Guide
Vegan, Gluten-Free, and Allergen-Friendly Alternatives

Creating dishes that accommodate various dietary preferences and restrictions can elevate your cooking while ensuring that everyone at your table feels included. This appendix provides a detailed substitution guide for vegan, gluten-free, and allergen-friendly alternatives, allowing you to adapt the recipes in this book with ease. Whether you're hosting a holiday gathering or preparing a treat for yourself, these substitutions will help you navigate common dietary concerns without compromising on flavor or texture.

General Substitution Principles

1. **Start Small:**
    ◦ When substituting ingredients, replace one component at a time to better understand its impact on the overall recipe.
2. **Flavor Balance:**
    ◦ Adjust spices, sweeteners, or liquids as needed to maintain the flavor and consistency of the original dish.
3. **Texture Matters:**
    ◦ Choose substitutes that mimic the texture and structure of the original ingredient for the best results.

Vegan Substitutions

1. Eggs

Eggs are commonly used for binding, leavening, or moisture. Here are vegan-friendly replacements:

- **Flax Egg or Chia Egg:**
    ◦ 1 tbsp ground flaxseed or chia seeds + 3 tbsp water = 1 egg.
    ◦ Let sit for 5-10 minutes to thicken. Ideal for muffins, cakes, and cookies.
- **Unsweetened Applesauce:**
    ◦ ¼ cup = 1 egg. Adds moisture and works well in dense baked goods.
- **Mashed Banana or Pumpkin Puree:**
    ◦ ¼ cup = 1 egg. Adds natural sweetness and moisture. Best for breads and pancakes.
- **Silken Tofu:**
    ◦ ¼ cup blended = 1 egg. Provides structure and works well in custards and dense desserts.

2. Dairy Products

- **Milk:**
    - Use almond, soy, oat, or coconut milk in a 1:1 ratio. Choose unsweetened varieties for savory recipes.
- **Butter:**
    - Replace with vegan butter or solid coconut oil in a 1:1 ratio. For baked goods, applesauce or mashed avocado can also work.
- **Heavy Cream:**
    - Coconut cream (the thick part of canned coconut milk) or cashew cream makes an excellent substitute.
- **Cheese:**
    - Use plant-based cheese alternatives. Nutritional yeast can add a cheesy flavor to sauces and savory dishes.

3. Honey

- Replace honey with maple syrup, agave nectar, or date syrup in equal amounts.

Gluten-Free Substitutions
1. All-Purpose Flour

- Use a gluten-free flour blend (commercial or homemade) in a 1:1 ratio. Look for blends containing xanthan gum or guar gum to mimic the elasticity of gluten.
- **Alternative Flours:**
    - **Almond Flour:** Adds richness but requires additional binding agents. Best for cookies and cakes.
    - **Coconut Flour:** Highly absorbent; use ¼ cup for every 1 cup of flour and increase liquid.
    - **Rice Flour:** Neutral flavor, ideal for pancakes or flatbreads.
    - **Oat Flour:** Adds a mild, nutty flavor. Ensure oats are certified gluten-free.

2. Bread Crumbs

- Replace with gluten-free breadcrumbs, crushed gluten-free crackers, or ground nuts like almonds or hazelnuts.

3. Pasta

- Swap regular pasta for gluten-free versions made from rice, quinoa, or lentils.

Allergen-Friendly Substitutions
1. Nuts

- Replace nuts with seeds like sunflower, pumpkin, or hemp seeds in granolas, salads, or baking.
- Use seed butters (sunflower seed butter or tahini) in place of peanut or almond butter.

2. Soy

- Replace soy milk with almond, oat, or rice milk.
- Use coconut aminos in place of soy sauce for marinades and stir-fries.

3. Corn

- Replace cornstarch with arrowroot powder, tapioca starch, or potato starch in a 1:1 ratio for thickening.
- Use rice tortillas or cassava-based alternatives in place of corn tortillas.

Baking-Specific Substitutions
1. Leavening Agents

- Replace self-rising flour with a mix of gluten-free flour, 1 ½ tsp baking powder, and ¼ tsp salt per cup.
- For baking powder, combine 1 tsp baking soda + 2 tsp cream of tartar.

2. Sweeteners

- Use coconut sugar, maple syrup, or monk fruit sweetener instead of white sugar. Adjust liquid if using syrups.

3. Gelatin

- Replace with agar-agar in a 1:1 ratio. Dissolve agar-agar in hot water for best results.

Savory Dish Substitutions
1. Stocks and Broths

- Replace chicken or beef broth with vegetable stock or water seasoned with soy sauce and nutritional yeast for depth.

2. Meat and Seafood

- **Ground Meat:** Replace with lentils, mushrooms, or plant-based meat crumbles.
- **Seafood:** Use hearts of palm, jackfruit, or tofu marinated in seaweed for a seafood-like flavor.

3. Oils and Fats

- Use olive oil, avocado oil, or grapeseed oil instead of butter or animal fats for roasting or sautéing.

Special Considerations for Allergies
Dairy-Free:

- Use coconut cream or oat-based products for creamy sauces and desserts.

Nut-Free:

- Swap almond milk or cashew cream with oat or rice milk. Use sunflower seed butter for spreads.

Egg-Free:

- Use aquafaba (the liquid from canned chickpeas) as a substitute for egg whites in meringues and whipped desserts.

Creating Your Own Substitution Plan

- **Step 1:** Identify the allergen or restriction in the recipe.
- **Step 2:** Choose a substitute that matches the ingredient's role (binding, leavening, flavor, or texture).
- **Step 3:** Test in small batches, adjusting liquid or dry ingredient ratios as needed.

Quick Reference Table

Ingredient	Vegan Substitute	Gluten-Free Substitute	Allergen-Friendly Substitute
Eggs	Flax egg, applesauce, tofu	N/A	N/A
Milk	Almond, oat, or soy milk	N/A	Rice or coconut milk
Flour	N/A	Gluten-free flour blend	Oat or almond flour (certified GF)
Butter	Vegan butter, coconut oil	N/A	Olive or avocado oil
Cheese	Nutritional yeast, vegan cheese	N/A	N/A
Bread Crumbs	N/A	GF breadcrumbs, nuts	Seed-based crumbs
Gelatin	Agar-agar	N/A	Agar-agar
Nuts	Seed alternatives (sunflower, etc.)	N/A	Sunflower, hemp, or pumpkin seeds

This substitution guide provides the tools to adapt any recipe in this book, ensuring inclusivity and creativity in your kitchen. No matter the dietary restriction, you can craft delicious, intergalactic meals that everyone will enjoy.

Allons-y!

Appendix C: Holiday Playlist

A Festive Doctor Who-Inspired Playlist for Cooking Sessions

Bring the magic of the *Doctor Who* universe into your kitchen with this curated holiday playlist, blending iconic music from the series, festive classics, and imaginative tunes that evoke the spirit of time and space. Whether you're baking, sautéing, or assembling your culinary masterpiece, this playlist will keep your cooking session energized, joyful, and perfectly on theme.

Doctor Who Soundtrack Selections

1. "I Am the Doctor" – Murray Gold

- **Why It Fits:** This triumphant and adventurous theme from the Eleventh Doctor era is the perfect energizer to kick off your cooking session. Let its heroic crescendos inspire creativity in the kitchen.

2. "The Shepherd's Boy" – Murray Gold

- **Why It Fits:** With its emotional swells and ethereal tones, this piece embodies the heart of the Doctor. It's perfect for moments of quiet focus, like decorating intricate pastries.

3. "Vale Decem" – Murray Gold

- **Why It Fits:** This hauntingly beautiful choral piece, played during the Tenth Doctor's regeneration, adds a touch of gravitas to your culinary endeavors. Use it for introspective moments while kneading dough or waiting for your cake to rise.

4. "Abigail's Song (Silence Is All You Know)" – Katherine Jenkins

- **Why It Fits:** This song from the Christmas episode *A Christmas Carol* is as heartwarming as a freshly baked pie. Play it while preparing festive desserts or decorating cookies.

5. "The Long Song" – Murray Gold

- **Why It Fits:** With its gentle melody and uplifting chorus, this piece inspires hope and determination, perfect for conquering a challenging recipe.

Festive Classics with a Doctor Who Twist
6. "Carol of the Bells" – Epic Orchestral Version

- **Why It Fits:** This dramatic, sci-fi-inspired rendition of the classic carol feels like it could accompany a Dalek invasion during the holidays. Perfect for high-energy moments like whisking or chopping.

7. "O Holy Night" – Instrumental Synthwave Cover

- **Why It Fits:** This version merges holiday tradition with futuristic vibes, creating an atmosphere that feels both festive and intergalactic.

8. "Jingle Bells" – Timey-Wimey Remix

- **Why It Fits:** A playful remix that incorporates sound effects reminiscent of the TARDIS materializing, making it a fun background track for assembling quirky treats like Jelly Baby Jellies.

9. "Silent Night" – Choral Version with Alien Ambience

- **Why It Fits:** This reimagined carol, infused with space-like soundscapes, feels like a hymn from Gallifrey itself. A soothing choice for reflective cooking moments.

10. "Deck the Halls" – Electric Violin Version

- **Why It Fits:** This lively interpretation adds a modern twist to a classic, much like the Doctor continually regenerates with new flair. Perfect for upbeat activities like decorating a cake or assembling an antipasto platter.

Imaginative Tracks for Intergalactic Vibes
11. "Clara's Theme" – Murray Gold

- **Why It Fits:** Light and whimsical, this piece evokes a sense of wonder and adventure, setting the tone for creative dishes like Gallifreyan Galaxy Pies.

12. "TARDIS Sound Effects" – Ambient Compilation

- **Why It Fits:** The iconic whooshing and humming sounds of the TARDIS provide a subtle and immersive backdrop to any cooking session. Great for when you're waiting for something to bake or boil.

13. "Astronomia" – Orchestral Remix

- **Why It Fits:** With its energetic beats and cosmic tones, this track captures the excitement of exploring the universe. Play it while multitasking in the kitchen.

14. "Doctor Disco" – From *The Husbands of River Song*

- **Why It Fits:** A playful track that brings lighthearted energy to your cooking session. Perfect for festive recipes like Regeneration Fruitcake or K-9 Canine Crunchers.

15. "Song for Ten" – Murray Gold

- **Why It Fits:** This nostalgic and celebratory song from *The Christmas Invasion* is a fan-favorite, ideal for reflecting on the joy of cooking and sharing food with loved ones.

Holiday Favorites for Time Travelers
16. "Have Yourself a Merry Little Christmas" – Crooner Style Remix

- **Why It Fits:** A comforting classic that pairs beautifully with slow moments, like glazing tarts or sipping tea as your bread bakes.

17. "Winter Wonderland" – Swing Jazz Cover

- **Why It Fits:** This upbeat rendition is perfect for dancing around the kitchen while preparing whimsical treats like Skaro Strawberry Tarts.

18. "Do They Know It's Christmas?" – Choir and Strings Remix

- **Why It Fits:** A heartfelt anthem that blends the holiday spirit with the grandeur of a *Doctor Who* soundtrack. Ideal for thoughtful cooking moments.

Playful Additions for Whovian Fun
19. "Don't Stop Me Now" – Queen (Featured in *The Magician's Apprentice*)

- **Why It Fits:** This energetic anthem captures the Doctor's unstoppable energy and determination. Blast it during moments when the kitchen chaos reaches its peak.

20. "Where No Man Has Gone Before" – Sci-Fi Orchestral Cover

- **Why It Fits:** Borrowing from the spirit of intergalactic adventure, this track keeps the energy high as you work on bold culinary creations.

Closing Tracks for a Celebratory Finish
21. "Twelve Days of Whomas" – Fan Parody

- **Why It Fits:** A humorous take on a holiday classic, this track is a great way to wind down after a long cooking session with a chuckle.

22. "Gallifrey Hymn" – Murray Gold

- **Why It Fits:** This solemn yet hopeful piece captures the grandeur and nostalgia of Gallifrey, making it the perfect final note as you admire your culinary creations.

How to Use This Playlist

- **Preparation Time:** Start with energetic tracks like "I Am the Doctor" and "Doctor Disco" to build momentum as you gather ingredients and start cooking.
- **Cooking Time:** Switch to soothing or atmospheric tracks like "Clara's Theme" or "Silent Night" for tasks that require focus and care.
- **Decorating Time:** Use playful tunes like "Deck the Halls (Electric Violin)" to keep the mood light and fun while decorating.
- **Serving Time:** End with celebratory or reflective tracks like "Song for Ten" or "Gallifrey Hymn" as you present your dishes.

This Doctor Who-inspired holiday playlist ensures that your cooking sessions are as exciting and dynamic as the Doctor's adventures through time and space. So, press play, grab your apron, and let the music transport you to a kitchen filled with festive, intergalactic joy.

Allons-y!

<u>**Message from the Author:**</u>

I hope you enjoyed this book, I love astrology and knew there was not a book such as this out on the shelf. I love metaphysical items as well. Please check out my other books:

-Life of Government Benefits

-My life of Hell

-My life with Hydrocephalus

-Red Sky

-World Domination:Woman's rule

-World Domination:Woman's Rule 2: The War

-Life and Banishment of Apophis: book 1

-The Kidney Friendly Diet

-The Ultimate Hemp Cookbook

-Creating a Dispensary(legally)

-Cleanliness throughout life: the importance of showering from childhood to adulthood.

-Strong Roots: The Risks of Overcoddling children

-Hemp Horoscopes: Cosmic Insights and Earthly Healing

- Celestial Hemp Navigating the Zodiac: Through the Green Cosmos

-Astrological Hemp: Aligning The Stars with Earth's Ancient Herb

-The Astrological Guide to Hemp: Stars, Signs, and Sacred Leaves

-Green Growth: Innovative Marketing Strategies for your Hemp Products and Dispensary

-Cosmic Cannabis

-Astrological Munchies

-Henry The Hemp

-Zodiacal Roots: The Astrological Soul Of Hemp

- Green Constellations: Intersection of Hemp and Zodiac

-Hemp in The Houses: An astrological Adventure Through The Cannabis Galaxy

-Galactic Ganja Guide

Heavenly Hemp

Zodiac Leaves

Doctor Who Astrology

Cannastrology

Stellar Satvias and Cosmic Indicas

<u>Celestial Cannabis: A Zodiac Journey</u>

AstroHerbology: The Sky and The Soil: Volume 1

AstroHerbology:Celestial Cannabis:Volume 2

Cosmic Cannabis Cultivation

The Starry Guide to Herbal Harmony: Volume 1

The Starry Guide to Herbal Harmony: Cannabis Universe: Volume 2

Yugioh Astrology: Astrological Guide to Deck, Duels and more

Nightmare Mansion: Echoes of The Abyss

Nightmare Mansion 2: Legacy of Shadows

Nightmare Mansion 3: Shadows of the Forgotten

Nightmare Mansion 4: Echoes of the Damned

The Life and Banishment of Apophis: Book 2

Nightmare Mansion: Halls of Despair

<u>Healing with Herb: Cannabis and Hydrocephalus</u>

<u>Planetary Pot: Aligning with Astrological Herbs: Volume 1</u>

Fast Track to Freedom: 30 Days to Financial Independence Using AI, Assets, and Agile Hustles

<u>Cosmic Hemp Pathways</u>

How to Become Financially Free in 30 Days: 10,000 Paths to Prosperity

Zodiacal Herbage: Astrological Insights: Volume 1

Nightmare Mansion: Whispers in the Walls

The Daleks Invade Atlantis

Henry the hemp and Hydrocephalus

10X The Kidney Friendly Diet

Cannabis Universe: Adult coloring book

Hemp Astrology: The Healing Power of the Stars

Zodiacal Herbage: Astrological Insights: Cannabis Universe: Volume 2

<u>Planetary Pot: Aligning with Astrological Herbs: Cannabis Universes: Volume 2</u>

Doctor Who Meets the Replicators and SG-1: The Ultimate Battle for Survival

Nightmare Mansion: Curse of the Blood Moon

<u>The Celestial Stoner: A Guide to the Zodiac</u>

Cosmic Pleasures: Sex Toy Astrology for Every Sign

Hydrocephalus Astrology: Navigating the Stars and Healing Waters

Lapis and the Mischievous Chocolate Bar

Celestial Positions: Sexual Astrology for Every Sign

Apophis's Shadow Work Journal: **:** A Journey of Self-Discovery and Healing

Kinky Cosmos: Sexual Kink Astrology for Every Sign

Digital Cosmos: The Astrological Digimon Compendium

Stellar Seeds: The Cosmic Guide to Growing with Astrology

Apophis's Daily Gratitude Journal

Cat Astrology: Feline Mysteries of the Cosmos

The Cosmic Kama Sutra: An Astrological Guide to Sexual Positions

Unleash Your Potential: A Guided Journal Powered by AI Insights
Whispers of the Enchanted Grove

Cosmic Pleasures: An Astrological Guide to Sexual Kinks
369, 12 Manifestation Journal
Whisper of the nocturne journal(blank journal for writing or drawing)
The Boogey Book
Locked In Reflection: A Chastity Journey Through Locktober
Generating Wealth Quickly:
How to Generate $100,000 in 24 Hours
Star Magic: Harness the Power of the Universe
The Flatulence Chronicles: A Fart Journal for Self-Discovery
The Doctor and The Death Moth
Seize the Day: A Personal Seizure Tracking Journal
The Ultimate Boogeyman Safari: A Journey into the Boogie World and Beyond
Whispers of Samhain: 1,000 Spells of Love, Luck, and Lunar Magic: Samhain Spell Book
Apophis's guides:
Witch's Spellbook Crafting Guide for Halloween
<u>Frost & Flame: The Enchanted Yule Grimoire of 1000 Winter Spells</u>
<u>The Ultimate Boogey Goo Guide & Spooky Activities for Halloween Fun</u>
Harmony of the Scales: A Libra's Spellcraft for Balance and Beauty
The Enchanted Advent: 36 Days of Christmas Wonders

Nightmare Mansion: The Labyrinth of Screams
Harvest of Enchantment: 1,000 Spells of Gratitude, Love, and Fortune for Thanksgiving
The Boogey Chronicles: A Journal of Nightly Encounters and Shadowy Secrets
The 12 Days of Financial Freedom: A Step-by-Step Christmas Countdown to Transform Your Finances
Sigil of the Eternal Spiral Blank Journal
A Christmas Feast: Timeless Recipes for Every Meal
Holiday Stress-Free Solutions: A Survival Guide to Thriving During the Festive Season
Yu-Gi-Oh! Holiday Gifting Mastery: The Ultimate Guide for Fans and Newcomers Alike
Holiday Harmony: A Hydrocephalus Survival Guide for the Festive Season
Celestial Craft: The Witch's Almanac for 2025 – A Cosmic Guide to Manifestations, Moons, and Mystical Events
Doctor Who: The Toymaker's Winter Wonderland
Tulsa King Unveiled: A Thrilling Guide to Stallone's Mafia Masterpiece
Pendulum Craft: A Complete Guide to Crafting and Using Personalized Divination Tools
Nightmare Mansion: Santa's Eternal Eve
Starlight Noel: A Cosmic Journey through Christmas Mysteries
The Dark Architect: Unlocking the Blueprint of Existence

Surviving the Embrace: The Ultimate Guide to Encounters with The Hugging Molly

The Enchanted Codex: Secrets of the Craft for Witches, Wiccans, and Pagans

Harvest of Gratitude: A Complete Thanksgiving Guide

Yuletide Essentials: A Complete Guide to an Authentic and Magical Christmas

Celestial Smokes: A Cosmic Guide to Cigars and Astrology

Living in Balance: A Comprehensive Survival Guide to Thriving with Diabetes Insipidus

Cosmic Symbiosis: The Venom Zodiac Chronicles

The Cursed Paw of Ambition

Cosmic Symbiosis: The Astrological Venom Journal

Celestial Wonders Unfold: A Stargazer's Guide to the Cosmos (2024-2029)

The Ultimate Black Friday Prepper's Guide: Mastering Shopping Strategies and Savings

Cosmic Sales: The Astrological Guide to Black Friday Shopping

Legends of the Corn Mother and Other Harvest Myths

Whispers of the Harvest: The Corn Mother's Journal

The Evergreen Spellbook

The Doctor Meets the Boogeyman

The White Witch of Rose Hall's SpellBook

The Gingerbread Golem's Shadow: A Study in Sweet Darkness

The Gingerbread Golem Codex: An Academic Exploration of Sweet Myths

The Gingerbread Golem Grimoire: Sweet Magicks and Spells for the Festive Witch

The Curse of the Gingerbread Golem

10-minute Christmas Crafts for kids

<u>Christmas Crisis Solutions: The Ultimate Last-Minute Survival Guide</u>

Gingerbread Golem Recipes: Holiday Treats with a Magical Twist

The Infinite Key: Unlocking Mystical Secrets of the Ages

Enchanted Yule: A Wiccan and Pagan Guide to a Magical and Memorable Season

Dinosaurs of Power: Unlocking Ancient Magick

Astro-Dinos: The Cosmic Guide to Prehistoric Wisdom

If you want solar for your home go here: https://www.harborsolar.live/apophisenterprises/

Get Some Tarot cards: https://www.makeplayingcards.com/sell/apophis-occult-shop

Get some shirts: https://www.bonfire.com/store/apophis-shirt-emporium/

<u>**Instagrams:**</u>
@apophis_enterprises,
@apophisbookemporium,
@apophisscardshop
Twitter: @apophisenterpr1
 Tiktok:@apophisenterprise
Youtube: @sg1fan23477, @FiresideRetreatKingdom
Hive: @sg1fan23477
CheeLee: @SG1fan23477

Podcast: Apophis Chat Zone: https://open.spotify.com/show/5zXbr-CLEV2xzCp8ybrfHsk?si=fb4d4fdbdce44dec

Newsletter: https://apophiss-newsletter-27c897.beehiiv.com/